CONTENTS

Shopping → p. 58

Entertainment → p. 64

Where to stay → p. 70

Street atlas → p. 102

DID YOU KNOW?

MAPS IN THE GUIDEBOOK

(104 A1) Page numbers
and coordinates refer to
the street atlas
(0) Site/address located off
the map
Coordinates are also given for
places that are not marked
on the street atlas
A public transportation map
can be found inside the back
cover

INSIDE BACK COVER:
PULL-OUT MAP →

PULL-OUT MAP 𝄔

(𝄔 A–B 2–3) Refers to the
removable pull-out map

The best MARCO POLO Insider Tips

Our top 15 Insider Tips

INSIDER TIP ▶ Built in Norway
The Norwegians are proud of their wooden buildings – and you can see why in the Arkitekturmuseet. Housed in Oslo's former Central Bank, you can marvel at three distinct eras in Nordic architectural history → **p. 37**

INSIDER TIP ▶ Sunset reloaded
If you go to the Monolith in Vigelandsparken early in the evening and look east, you can watch the reflection of the sunset in the façades of houses opposite → **p. 41**

INSIDER TIP ▶ Rack and ruins
Minneparken: Where the bishop's palace now is, was the religious centre of power in medieval Oslo too → **p. 44**

INSIDER TIP ▶ Tiny Ida
The fossil of the 60cm-tall primate called Ida in the Naturhistorisk Museum is considered to be the 'missing link' in human evolution → **p. 46**

INSIDER TIP ▶ Picnic on an iceberg
Fancy going up in the world without risking your neck? The roof of the new opera house is a thrilling spot for a bite to eat with a view of the fjord and Oslo's up-and-coming centre → **p. 47**

INSIDER TIP ▶ The little brother and eroticism
The Emanuel Vigeland Museum: The fresco in the mausoleum designed by Gustav Vigeland's younger brother is a homage to the Renaissance and to eroticism. But if you blush, nobody will notice – the light is very dim → **p. 47**

INSIDER TIP ▶ As delicious as at the big brother's
Dr. Kneipp's Vinbar is the little brother to Markveien Mat & Vinhus and the perfect place for a glass of good wine and a delicious meal. And even better – it is less expensive than its sibling (photo above) → **p. 53**

BEST OF ...

● *A stroll past works of art*
Gustav Vigeland's mass of sculptures on display in the open attract millions of visitors – not because it is free of charge but because the monumental figures in Vigeland Park are incredibly impressive → p. 41

● *The Changing of the Guard*
The Changing of the Guard takes place every day at 1.30pm. When office workers are casually returning from their lunch break, the afternoon shift takes over outside the Royal Palace in accordance with strict military protocol (photo) → p. 32

● *Looking down on the city from above*
Those with a head for heights should take the glass lift up to the 34th floor of the Plaza Hotel where you will be rewarded with one of the best views of Oslo from the 34 Skybar. And it won't cost you a penny either → p. 40

● *Open-air concerts*
If you don't have to pay for a concert, the music can sometimes sound that much better. And when it is in the open on a balmy summer's night? Perfect! Throughout the summer, free rock, pop and folk concerts are regularly held on the square outside the city hall, for example → p. 68

● *Walking above the fjord*
An architectonic masterpiece with a social component. Everybody should be able to get their enjoyment from the magnificent white marble opera house. You can wander around on the roof, find a quiet corner, unpack your picnic lunch and take in the view over the city and the fjord → p. 47

● *Cool off*
... and have a swim in the middle of the city. Where can you do that? Below Nydal dam the Akerselva forms a pond surrounded by open grassy areas for sunbathing – the perfect place to relax those weary limbs after all that sightseeing. And it's free → p. 81

●●●● Dots in guidebook refer to 'Best of ...' tips

● *Beam me up*

The Holmenkollen ski jump curves elegantly away from the slope and forms the focal point of a magnificent ski arena which is both a major landmark and the heart of Norway's national sport. A high-speed lift takes you up the tower, from which you have an unbeatable view, almost as quickly as the skiers speed down the jump → p. 48

● *Read and be read*

Along with the Icelanders, the Norwegians have the greatest appetite for literature of any nation in the world and Oslo is proud of having a proper literature building where readings and cultural debates are held. There is also a literature café where many guests nowadays sit with iPads in front of them → p. 67

● *Traditional Norwegian gourmet fare*

Apart from a large number of regular guests, inquisitive and hungry tourists also find there way to this pinnacle of perfection – Mat & Vinhus – and are rewarded with excellent Norwegian delicacies such as reindeer and herring specialities (photo) → p. 57

● *Midsummer's night in the park*

Join the locals in Frogner Park and party the 'white night' through 'til dawn in the middle of the city to the sound of the chink of glasses and strumming of guitars. People crowd around the Monolith in Vigeland Sculpture Park to catch a glimpse of the remaining ruddy light of one day and the sun rising early the next → p. 86

● *Seeing with the eyes of a child*

Child-friendly Oslo even has a *Museum for International Children's Art* with a wide variety of shapes and colours depicting how children see the world. And children can join in everything too – while adults are only allowed to watch → p. 84

● *Herr Nilsen sets the tone*

Oslo is a bastion of jazz and the jazz club *Herr Nilsen* is at its very heart. Here you can listen to traditional jazz of a high standard played live almost every evening. During the breaks, pints are downed along with memories, future plans and masses of shoptalk → p. 68

ONLY IN

BEST OF ...

- *Clay time*
  Create you own pottery objects at *Glazed & Amused*. You can knead and model clay, experiment with different colours and have a lot of fun for two hours on end → p. 62

- *Coffee to stay*
  If you get caught by the rain in Frogner Park, head for the little café *Valkyrien Te & Kaffe* where the tram line terminates. There's not much room but it has huge windows and the wafting scent of far-off countries. Some claim that the best coffee in Oslo is to be found here → p. 52

- *Hop off to the 'museum island'*
  Norway's eventful maritime history can be traced without getting your feet wet on *Bygdøy* peninsula, which can be reached on a small ferry. Marvel at Roald Amundsen's single-masted sailing boat and original Viking ships (photo) → p. 81

- *Art cooperative*
  The *Kunstnerforbundet* holds temporary art and craft exhibitions of works by more than 300 Norwegian artists which are also for sale → p. 59

- *Go for a ride*
  Keep dry by taking a trip on tram no. 12 from Majorstuen on Frogner Park to the district of Kjelsås in the north. You will have a wonderful view of the city and Oslo Fjord to the south between the stops Satnatoriet and Glads vei → p. 23

- *Shop in the dry*
  The traditional department store *Steen & Strøm* that stocks Norwegian and international labels is well worth a visit. When your credit card has been exploited to the limit, finish the day in the brasserie on the 6th floor → p. 60

RAIN

RELAX AND CHILL OUT
Take it easy and spoil yourself

● *The glamour of yesteryear*
Those who consider themselves anybody have lunch or at least a drink in the bar in the Hotel Bristol. Sink into one of the chesterfields, browse the well-stocked bookshelves or simply listen to the soft piano music – not a bad life! → **p. 74**

● *The heart of Oslo*
In winter it's an ice rink; in the summer a small park with lots of benches. The little square *Studenterlunden* is squeezed in between Karl Johans gate, the National Theatre and Stortinget. The perfect place to unwind and people-watch → **p. 28**

● *Waffles in the henhouse*
The further you go up the Akerselva river, the quieter and more rural it becomes. You ultimately come to a waterfall and a red-painted cottage. Tuck into a delicious Norwegian waffle in *Hønse Lovisas hus* and simply switch off → **p. 80**

● *Woody Holmenkollen*
Just spoil yourself properly in the *Holmenkollen Park Hotell* – in front of the fire in the hotel bar, in the luxuriously appointed spa or in one of the wood panelled restaurants → **p. 72**

● *Frascati on the fjord*
Enjoy a glass of chilled white wine and watch the sunset from *Hukodden* beach restaurant and marvel at the summer light over Oslo Fjord that seems especially bright here → **p. 33**

● *Secret hideaway*
Right in the city centre and yet idyllically rural. At *Asylet* you can escape the hustle and bustle of the capital and unwind in the restaurant's inner courtyard with a glass of beer, a snack and a book. And as it's open to the heavens, smokers feel at home here too (photo) → **p. 55**

INTRODUCTION

DISCOVER OSLO!

Looking at Oslo from the water, you can see how the city cosily nestles between green hills. Its skyline is a real mixture of all sorts with a container port on one side and a marina on the other. In between are the new opera house sparkling in the sun, massive Akershus Fortress standing proud on a promontory, the square towers of the red brick city hall and the promenade Aker Brygge. The whole dynamism of the Norwegian capital is spread out in front of you: industry and leisure, culture and history, politics and pleasure. Strolling through the streets visitors soon discover that everything is quite modest in size – almost provincial – and that both the people of Oslo as well as its wonderful setting between the fjord and *fjell* dictate the pace of life in the city. Covering 175mi² – about a third the size of London – it has masses of space for a population of under 900,000. Half the area is forested and there are more than 300 lakes. This is highly valued by the people of Oslo who love their *friluftsliv*. Being out in the fresh air is something taken for granted by Norwegians. If you ask them what they like most about their city, they answer Nordmarka or Østmarka, depending on where

Photo: The sailing ship Christian Radich in Oslo Fjord with the City Hall behind

they live, and mean the wooded belt around the city. The train ride up to 500m (1640ft) above sea level, to Holmenkollen, to Voksenkollen (where you can hire skis) or to Frognerseter, followed by a hike on foot or skis through the forest, is a perfectly normal Sunday afternoon occupation and can be highly recommended to the more active visitor. And don't be surprised when you see people in a street café in Oslo in their skiing or hiking garb, rucksacks at their feet, enjoying a refreshing pint having just returned to civilisation.

The fjord with its countless bays lures the locals out in the summer. Sailing boats and motor launches sail and chug around, cheek by jowl, right up to the moorings in the city centre which is buzzing with beer stands and sunbathers who, dark glasses on their noses and sun protection factor 20 on their skin, gaze out across the fjord. Far-reaching views go hand in hand with living in Oslo which is why houses on the sides of hills cost treble the average price. There are plenty of boats to take tourists off to the islands and skerries to sunbathe. Those in the know treasure that special bonus offered by a trip on the fjord in winter too. When the diffuse light, laden with frost, descends over the capital city framed by snowy hills, Oslo from the water becomes a mystical place indeed.

Oslo is Norway's only major city and yet it is anything but a metropolis with no trace of the frantic pace of other capitals. Nevertheless there are a lot of cars, shops and buskers that all raise the decibel level, with a few skaters weaving their way around the pedestrians. But nobody screams and shouts or loses their temper. The few tables

The Botanic Garden is like the icing on a cake in a city that is bursting with green everywhere

and chairs outside restaurants and cafés are always occupied whatever the weather thanks to patio heaters and woollen blankets.

Everything seems leisurely here. Norwegians would never dream of showing their anger by shouting or sounding their horns and this reserved attitude characterises life in the capital too. This is even emphasised by the architecture as street canyons are always broken up by green spaces. Statistically, 95% of the urban population have a park within 300m of their home. The many squares and parks in the city are there for people to stroll through or sit on a bench and relax, watching the world drift by. And it is certainly no coincidence that the centre of Oslo is not the main station or the palace, but *Studenterlunden* park between the parliament building and the National Theatre. The former *campus*, a rectangular park full of benches, is Oslo's meeting place *par excellence* – for locals and visitors alike. In winter it is transformed into an ice rink that is popular not only with the younger generation in the capital.

> **The centre of Oslo is a park**

Visitors to Oslo will quickly notice how old and new buildings often fail to harmonise and how the city has few architecturally homogenous districts. Traffic was given much too much consideration in urban planning schemes up to the turn of the millennium and this is not helped by the general appearance of many a multi-storey car park. The rethinking of the past ten years however has done Oslo a lot of good. The main arteries have disappeared underground and the city is rapidly opening up towards the fjord. Promenades along the shoreline and squares known as *allmenning* in Norwegian are making a lasting change to the city's appearance from the water, stretching from Bjørvika Bay to the popular entertainment district Aker Brygge. This

is where the new National Gallery and Munch Museum are being built which, along with the opera house, will give Oslo a new skyline. What is growing up around the opera house – the 'European Building of the Year 2008' that can be seen from afar and exudes a welcoming openness – could well turn the city into a true metropolis, at least architecturally. Whatever the case, it will underline Oslo's claim as a cultural city to be reckoned with.

A large percentage of Norway's culture budget of just under £1 billion (1.5 billion US$) is earmarked for the capital. The city itself spends around £50 million (80 million US$) on subsidies for theatre, music, literature and art – on average that means more than £78 (123 US$) per person! The opera house and the Munch Museum

benefit from this just as hundreds of music clubs and small theatres. Some 6000 concerts are held in Oslo every year and there is always something for every taste. There are almost 1000 bands in the city – a blossoming environment from which international stars emerge from time to time.

Tension between the capital and the different regions

Norway has a population of 5 million, 900,000 of whom live in the greater Oslo area. That is a considerable number and, bearing the city's position in the southeast corner of the country, it comes as no surprise that a smouldering conflict has always existed between the capital and the rest of the country. Outside the capital it is generally rumoured that the people of Oslo don't know that Vestfjord is in the north of Norway whereas Nordfjord is in the west. And they also have to put up with being accused of arrogance and considering themselves the centre of the universe although, in actual fact, they are heavily dependent economically on profit-generating regions. Oslo is not only the seat of the government and most state authorities but also of all national daily newspapers. The tension between the capital and the different regions was particularly apparent in the two EU referendums held in 1972 and 1994. On both occasions, the people of Oslo considered themselves citizens of the EU – and were certain of success. However, they had to accept that Norwegians living in the west, the centre and the north blocked the route to Brussels.

The conflict between government and governed is largely historical. Between 1536 and 1814, when Norway belonged to Denmark and was ruled from Copenhagen, *Christiania* – as Oslo was then called – was the main supporting pillar of the land of the midnight sun. While throughout the country fishermen, farmers and the trade with their produce kept the wheels of the economy oiled, the city on Oslo Fjord was dominated by representatives of the Crown and by civil servants who received their pay from Copenhagen. The two relatively recent EU referendums once again underlined these contrasting historical poles. The people of Oslo have to live under the critical eye of their fellow countrymen but this has not had any effect on the city-dwellers' self-confidence at all. They have got used to palming off any disparaging remarks with a smile. However, they still have a certain inferiority complex – which also has historical roots – with regard to other Nordic capitals, Stockholm in particular. Nevertheless, the country's wealth after 40 years of oil and gas production has changed the city and its inhabitants. It is seething with exclusive restaurants and expensive cars – and with different Norwegian dialects. The country's wealth is reflected in particular in the seemingly haphazard construction of skyscrapers around the main station. This is not a place for a quiet moment, this is where the financial elite have their say. Just a few hundred yards away, nothing of this pretentiousness whatsoever can be found in the restaurants, cafés and bars of Grønland or Grünerløkka. Things here seem more established, a little frayed around the edges, but charmingly intimate. A place to get to know new people and live happily side by side where you will always hear a 'Nice to see you, how are things?' According to international surveys, the Norwegians have an extremely high life expectancy, a very high standard of living and high educational standards –

The people of Oslo go outside whenever possible to bask in the sun in cafés, parks and squares

and they are the most optimistic nation in the world. The people of Oslo radiate a worry-free attitude – something that is an essential part of the locals' attitude to life. Even the tragic events of 22 July, 2011 have not changed this, when a 32-year-old Norwegian set off a large car bomb in front of the parliament building in Oslo city centre that killed eight. He then carried out a barbaric massacre in a summer camp attended by Norways's Young Socialists on the island of Utøya in Lake Tyrifjorden, killing 69 mostly young people. Despite the intense shock and overwhelming grief for the victims, a determination could be sensed from the outset to maintain values so important to the Norwegians: openness, solidarity and the right to live freely.

> **Important values: openness, solidarity and the right to live freely**

Oslo is and will always be a city at odds with itself. That something is always being built can be seen as an expression of restlessness by some while others praise its dynamism. That Oslo is on the edge of Europe is made up for by a pulsating, trendy nightlife scene and the many internationally renowned restaurants and chefs. That, in the capital of a country people think of as being puritanical, tolerance is of utmost importance, is very much in keeping with the fundamental attitude of the Norwegians to 'live and let live'. And that the Norwegians themselves regard their capital city with a generous portion of scepticism does not stop the people of Oslo from being immensely proud of where they live. Contradictory in other words, but exciting even at a second glance. There are many good reasons to approach this city without preconceived ideas and to be drawn by its own special magic.

WHAT'S HOT

1 Grønland

'In' district There is something exciting to discover on virtually every street corner in Grønland, the city's latest trendy district. Labels such as *3rdhand* created by the designers Anne Brit Opdahl and Laura Armonaite can be found here *(Markveien 58)*, artists sell their works in *Galerie 0047 (Schweigaardsgate 340, photo)* and provide inspiration for the younger crowd. And after sunset everyone meets up in *Gloria Flames*. Concerts, cool drinks and a roof terrace make this the perfect venue *(Grønland 18)*.

Daring fashions

2

Racy Oslo's fashion designers never do things by halves. Prepare yourself for some extravagent designs – for example from *Moods of Norway (Akersgata 18, www.moodsofnorway.no, photo)* or Cecilie Melli, who creates whacky accessories *(Nedre Slottsgate 15, www.ceciliemelli.com)*. The big designer names can be found at *Den Dama* and more recently at *Hassan og Den Dama (Frognerveien 4 and Skovveien 4, dendama.com)*.

Disc golf

3

Blooming baskets Frisbees in Oslo's parks aren't necessarily thrown from one person to another. More often than not they now end up in a basket. Disc golf is the name of the game and baskets are popping up everywhere like mushrooms. There are nine alone in *Frognerpark (www.frognerfrisbeeklubb.no)*, double that number in the leisure park in Ekeberg where the disc golf club *Ekeberg Sendeplateklubb* regularly lets things fly *(Ekebergsletta, www.ekebergsk.com, photo)*. After all, members want to be fit to take on the frisbee champs *EZ Ultimate*. Guest players are welcome too *(www.ezultimate.no)*.

Eat green

Local and delicious The founders of *Food Story* are green through and through. Not only is the food in their restaurants and café-shops organic but it is also produced locally. In its branches in Grünerløkka there are not only sandwiches and salads but also delicious mussels and lamb with wild herbs *(Thorvald Meyers gate 61, photo)*. One real oasis can be found in a quiet courtyard: *Kolonihagen*, an organic delivery service, has brought a hairdresser, baker, florist, café and greengrocer together to form a real organic idyll in the city centre *(Frogner-veien 33)*. Whereas *Food Story* and *Kolonihagen* serve meat, the *Spisestedet* restaurant is both organic and vegetarian – and delicious too *(Hjelms gate 3)*.

Chameleons

Club meets café The people of Oslo tend to stay put when they have discovered a nice place to be. Perhaps that has something to do with cafés that turn into clubs in the evening. In cosy *Illegal Burger*, meat from the grill is served in breadrolls during the day and records spun on turntables in the evening *(Møllergata 23)*. You'll find yourself in the right place around the clock at *Café con Bar* too. The music is turned up after the sun goes down, cocktails are shaken and a youngish crowd floats around between the bar and the cushy sofas *(Brugata 11)*. Culture doesn't get overlooked either: *Galleri Pan* is a combination of art location, restaurant, winebar and concert venue *(St. Olavs gate 7, www.panoslo.no)*. And even the more profane things in life double up too. As for example the friendly café-cum-laundrette *(Café Laundromat, Underhaugsveien 2, photo)*.

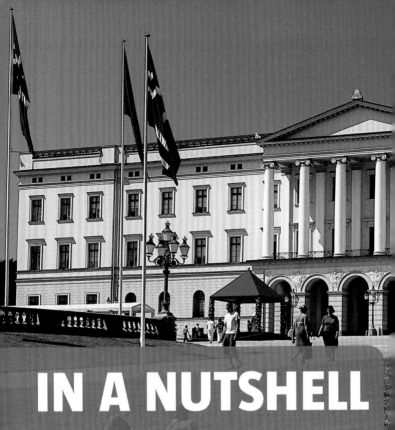

IN A NUTSHELL

ATTACKS ON 22 JULY, 2011

On Friday 22 July, 2011, the kingdom of Norway experienced a nightmare that horrified the world and plunged the whole country in the north of Europe into grief. A 32-year-old Norwegian carried out two terrorist attacks, aimed precisely at the heart of Norway's social democracy and as such at society in general. After having ignited a 500kg (1100lb) car bomb in front of the parliament building on Johann Nygaardsvolds plass, that caused enormous damage and claimed the lives of eight victims, the assassin drove some 30 minutes to the west to Lake Tyrifjorden and crossed to the island of Utøya dressed in a policeman's uniform. At that time, Norway's Young Socialists (AUF) were on a summer camp there. The assassin shot 69 participants at close range – the youngest victim was only 14 years old. Around 70 other youths suffered injuries, many of which were severe. The killer surrendered at the scene of the crime. Politicians and the general public reacted by reaffirming Norway's position as a free country whose values are to be upheld.

DESIGN & FASHION

That Norway is not at the trend-

Football, jazz, sport – the people of Oslo are sociable and like being outside, especially on midsummer's night

setting centre of Europe can also be felt in the field of design and fashion. However, there are any number of young and daring designers for whom Paris, London and Milan are too far away. There are also lots of possibilities for studying as well as exhibition spaces and sales rooms, inviting shops which are delight to browse around and where you can marvel at and buy cleverly designed articles. There is even an internationally renowned designer hotel. However, few designers manage to get a foothold in the mainstream European scene. The fashion designers at *Moods of Norway* are exceptions, as are the innovative lighting designer *Northern Lightning* and Ørjan Djønne and Marius Sveen of *Bare Møbler* with their sturdy but original seats and seating arrangements.

FOOTBALL PUBS

Expensive beer seems to taste better when watching a football match. Although the national team, players and clubs in Norway barely play a role in international sport, football's popularity can be seen everywhere throughout Oslo. Since the early days of television, Norwegians have been fans of English football in particular – and of course this tradition has to be nurtured. Visitors to the Norwegian capital shouldn't be surprised when they come across locals watching top British clubs several times a week on large screens in Oslo's pubs – which by the way often have English names too.

JAZZ

For decades now Oslo has been at the centre of the internationally acclaimed Norwegian jazz scene. At the beginning of the 1980s, it was the singer Karin Krog and saxophonist Jan Garbarek who paved the way for talented Norwegian musicians. And in 1983, one of the best recording studios in the world was set up in Oslo: *Recorded at Rainbow Studio, Oslo. Engineer: Jan Erik Kongshaug* is an absolute guarantee for quality in jazz music. Many of the best international jazz labels have Norwegian groups and soloists on their lists of records. These also help ensure that concerts in the capital's many venues are well attended. *Bare Jazz* in the heart of the city *(Grensen 8)* with a virtually unlimited range of classical and modern recordings and the *Nasjonal Jazzscene* in Victoria, right on Oslo's main boulevard Karl Johans gate *(www.nasjonaljazzscene.no)*, form the backbone of the music scene.

MARIA MENA & CO.

Super soft pop ballads from the cool north. The daughter of a drummer has music in her blood and the makings of an international star. Maria Mena's break-

through came in 2005 with her song 'Apparently Unaffected' which sold more than 250,000 copies. The young Oslo girl's very personal texts are particularly popular in Holland and Germany, but she is also known in the USA and has been a guest on David Letterman's late night talk show. The singer Marit Larsen, a great fan of Joni Mitchell, among others, is now emerging from Maria Mena's shadow in a big way and is now considered as the Norwegian capital's up-and-coming star.

MIDSUMMER'S NIGHT

The summer solstice is something to be celebrated properly and to the full. After all, you can always sleep as much as you like when summer is over! Everyone takes a holiday or at least has the weekend free, if at all possible, and the night is turned into day. The missing night's sleep is made up for during the day on the grass in a park in the middle of the city. This is especially the case in the night from the 23–24 June when the people in

During midsummer's night the sky over Oslo stays light and almost every bed empty

the capital have bonfires and barbecues along the shore of Olso Fjord to celebrate midsummer's night. The sun does actually disappear for a few hours but the city doesn't really quieten down. Many more people than normal are up and about until way past midnight. A more or less sober crowd along the party strip, Aker Brygge, and people on sailing boats moored in front of the city hall party away until the sun starts to rise. Unfortunately, alcohol consumption does have its effect as the night draws on. Visitors to the city may not find this much fun. The best way to counteract this is to join in or take a boat to the quiet skerries out in Oslo Fjord. Or, of course, you could even go to bed.

MONARCHY

Although the ancestry of the Norwegian Crown goes back to the time of the Vikings, Norway's monarchy is actually quite young. After more than 400 years under the foreign rule of the Danes (up until 1814) and just less than a century under the Swedish Crown, the country had to import a prince from Denmark in 1905 who then ascended the Norwegian throne after a referendum had been held. To this day, the popularity of the royal family remains unbroken. Harald V, Crown Prince Haakon Magnus and Princess Märtha Louise have all married commoners and nobody has any problems with this. The monarch and his children are even respected by republicans in the country. While the Crown Prince pursued the traditional career of a future king, training to be an officer and studying, and has already represented the country both at home and abroad accompanied by his wife, Crown Princess Mette-Marit, his older sister, Märtha Louise, has – literally – taken an alternative path. After training to be a physiotherapist abroad, and after marrying the author Ari Behn in 2002, she relinquished the title 'Her Royal Highness' that same year to be able to continue working independently in the field of culture. She has appeared on television as

a storyteller and travelled around Norway on tour during Advent. Märtha Louise founded a centre for alternative medical treatment in 2007 and, according to her own words, can communicate with angels and animals – something that caused quite a stir not only in the Norwegian press.

NOBEL PRIZE

Oslo is at the centre of global media interest twice a year – and it was a Swede who was behind this in the first place. The industrialist and businessman Alfred Nobel (1833–1896) from Stockholm specified in his will that the Nobel Peace Prize winner – unlike the four other Nobel Prizes awarded for Physics, Chemistry, Medicine and Literature – be selected and awarded by a Norwegian Nobel committee, appointed by the Stortinget. For this reason there is a Nobel Institute in Oslo and the *Nobels Fredssenter* information centre near Aker Brygge.

Every year on the second Friday in October, the chairman of the Norwegian Nobel Committee announces the recipient of the Nobel Peace Prize at 11am on the dot. The prize is awarded on 10 December, the date of Alfred Nobel's death, when the medal and a check that at present is for 10 million Swedish kronor (£950,000 or 1.5m US$) is presented in a ceremony at Oslo city hall.

OSLO FJORD

It would be hard to imagine Norway's capital without its fjord. It is the gateway to the city, a sailor's paradise, a heavily frequented stretch of water and a unique recreational area all rolled into one. Approx. 2 million people live on or near the two shores of this arm of the sea that forms part of Skagerrak strait. Due to its location it has often had to struggle for survival. Settlements, industry and traffic have effected the quality of the water, especially in the so-called Inner Oslo Fjord. This starts at Drøbaksund, which is just 1km (about ½mi) wide, and reaches as far as Oslo city hall over a maximum length of 7km (4½mi).

Sailing boats and motor launches have to jiggle backwards and forwards to avoid each other on this stretch of water in the summer. Countless, very expensive cabins are dotted about on the skerries and rocky islets. But none of this has damaged Oslo Fjord's reputation as it has a firm place in the hearts of the people of Oslo.

KEEP FIT!

Oslo's best-known area for people to walk and jog can be reached by taking tram no. 3 from the centre (alighting at Sognsvann). A quick run around *Sognsvann Lake* is a perfect tour – close enough to the city centre while being out in the forests of Norway at the same time. The route is a mere 3.3km (2mi) long. The fresh air and the open countryside come free of charge too. For those who don't or can't jog, the well-maintained gravel path is suitable for bikes as well. Wheelchair users can also follow this route around the lake without any problems. And if you want to go further, just turn off the way-marked path and explore the Marka woods. Long-distance runners can devise their own jogging course to last as many miles as they want.

Elsewhere a form of public transport – in Oslo the *trikken* is a love affair as well

SPORT

There are some myths that survive the course of time – 'Norwegians are sporty' being one of them. And since Oslo has had to defend its reputation as a sports' capital since the Winter Olympic Games in 1952, people are actively involved attracting locals and visitors to the city to do sport at professional and amateur levels in the summertime as well. The athletics meeting in Bislett Stadium one Friday in June has been a grand-prix event since 1998. The international marathon continues to break the record of the number of participants registered from year to year and the Holmenkollen Relay, with more than 2000 teams and more than 30,000 participants, has advanced to become one of the largest running events in the world.

TRAMS

Perhaps it's because Oslo is the only city in Norway which has a tram system at all, or perhaps it's because the *Trikken* network serves the main urban area of Oslo so well. Whatever the reason: the locals love their trams. The blue carriages that are anything but state-of-the-art more or less struggle along from east to west, with every line passing through the main station in the city centre *en route*. Anyone wanting to get to know Oslo and its people in a relaxed way while staying warm and dry can – for a surprising low fare – should buy a day ticket (valid 24 hours) and travel from one highlight to the next and back and forth. ● Line 12 offers particularly attractive views.

The first trams in Oslo were horse-drawn from 1875 until 1894. The network was electrified in 1900. Now, 72 carriages run up and down the lines 11, 12, 13, 17, 18 and 19. A new line is being planned to the opera house and along Oslo Fjord. And before this decade is over, a new fjord line is expected to be completed to serve the far western section of the city.

THE PERFECT DAY
Oslo in 24 hours

08:30am CAFFÈ LATTE WITH A VIEW OF THE PALACE

You can start your day with breakfast at *Wayne's Coffee* → p. 53 near where the ferry from Kiel to Oslo comes in – generously filled sandwiches, delicious cakes and arguably the best *caffè latte* in Oslo. When the weather is good, choose a table outside. Diagonally opposite is the Nobel Institute; beyond it is the royal park.

10:00am VILLAS AND PALACES

Whoever wants to know what the *Royal Palace* → p. 31 (photo left) is like inside should buy a ticket for the one-hour guided tour in good time. Afterwards, head for the embassy district backing onto the royal park with its imposing, elegant townhouses lined up harmoniously next to one another. There is less traffic in *Frogner* → p. 38 and many more things to look at, such as beautifully decorated villas, ornamental bay windows and the one or other cosy café. You can reach Frogner Park along Frognerveien, Niels Juels gate and Gyldenløves gate.

11:00am GIANTS IN THE PARK

The central feature is the collection of monumental sculptures by Gustav Vigeland in the section of the park known as *Vigelandsparken* → p. 41. You don't have to like this type of art and the exaggerated human forms, but the avenue up to the *Monolith* at the centre of the collection invites visitors to have a look at the figures on both sides on the way. *Frogner Park* → p. 38 itself is the city's largest recreational area. Frisbees spin through the air, the strum of guitars can be heard and the wafting smell of barbecues is in the air – the perfect place to lie down and gaze at the sky over Oslo. If the weather is not up to it, pay a visit instead to the recently modernised *Vigeland Museum* → p. 41.

01:00pm UP, UP AND AWAY

From Majorstuen station take line no. 1 to Frognerseter. The tram crawls up to *Holmenkollen* → p. 48 the ski arena which boasts a new ski jump since 2010. After a visit to the ski musuem (photo right) and to the tower which offers spectacular views, you can head for the forests of Nordmarka – or save this outing for another day. Down in the city below

Get to know some of the most dazzling, exciting and relaxing facets of Oslo – all in a single day

there is still a lot to explore. Take tram no. 1 again to Ellingsrudåsen and relax on the 40-minute journey to Tøyen.

03:00pm THE GREAT MASTER MUNCH AND THE PRIMATE IDA

The *Munch Museum* → p. 45 is the best way to get to know the work of the great Expressionist. The world's largest collection of paintings and graphic works by Norway's most famous artist needs some time; the café in the building can provide the necessary sustenance of a physical kind after all the works of art. For those still up to visiting another museum, head over the road to the *Natural History Museum* → p. 46, where the 47 million-year-old primate, Ida – assumed to be the 'missing link' between the animal kingdom and mankind – is on display alongside dinosaurs and other creatures which lived all that time ago.

10:30am DINE LIKE A NORWEGIAN

Now it's time for a proper meal and, so that you can enjoy something typically Norwegian, it's off to *Olympen mat og vinhus* → p. 57 in the less pristine district of Grønland – either on foot or with the line no. 1 to Grønland. Dark oak panelling, long wooden tables, waiters in black waistcoats and the biggest choice of different types of beer in the city provide the setting for a hearty 3-course meal, preferably with some fish.

09:00pm DRINKS WITH A VIEW OF THE FJORD

Finish your day in Oslo where both tourists and locals most like to go on a summer's evening – to the promenade at *Aker Brygge* → p. 29 (photo above) with schooners bobbing about in front of you. This is where the city opens up to the fjord and where pubs stay open until the early hours. The sun will already be quite high in the sky by the time the last Viking has found his way back to his bunk.

Trams to starting point: 12, 13
Stop: Solli plass. A day pass (valid 24 hrs; 75 NOK) is worth it if you are going to go by tram at least 3 times!

SIGHTSEEING

CITY WHERE TO START

(113 E2) (*H4–5*) Rådhus-plassen: Standing on this square you have the fjord and quays behind and the bulky city hall in front of you. From here, Oslo's sights spread out like a fan – many of which are within easy walking distance. This is where sightseeing tours start too. Tram no. 12 runs to the station where all underground, tram and regional lines converge, as well as the bus terminal. There are several car parks to the east and west of the square.

If you were to imagine Oslo without the fjord and the wooded hills to the north, the city could perhaps seem a bit dull – a palace, a world-famous ski jump, a park with an impressive collection of sculptures, a massive city hall and the recent addition of a white marble opera house right on the water. So that's all there is, is it? No, it isn't! Sometimes you just need to change your viewpoint to discover what makes this capital city so surprising and special.

Drive a few miles to the northwest, to ❄ INSIDERTIP *Kragstøtten* above the Holmenkollen ski jump site, to the best viewpoint in Oslo. On a clear summer's

---

Photo: View from Pipervika of Akershus Festning

A red city hall, a white opera house and green parks – Oslo's sights spread out like a colourful fan offset by the blue of the fjord

day you can peer out over the fjord that, somewhere to the south, disappears between the islands, and gaze across to the slopes to the west and east with the whole city spread out at your feet.

The correct pronunciation of Oslo is 'Ush-lu' and the valley basin down below, locally called *Oslo Gryta* – the cauldron – has a few surprises in store: manorial farmsteads and cottages, relics of Oslo's days

as a farming community, huge industrial buildings now occupied by cultural organisations, elegant town houses and a varied and vibrant cultural scene. Districts of wooden houses have even survived into the 21st century in Oslo – in the west most are painted white and occupied by the wealthy; in the east they are generally red and inhabited by workers. Walks through the different districts in Oslo are

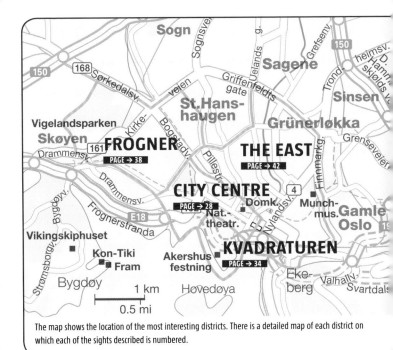

The map shows the location of the most interesting districts. There is a detailed map of each district on which each of the sights described is numbered.

encounters with the city's history and the changes necessitated by the continuously growing capital. The best idea is to climb up above the city and take in the view. And when you go exploring Norway's capital, the tram *(trikken)* is the perfect means of transport – apart from walking. Trams run to all parts of the city and when travelling from one sight to the next you can also gain a few impressions of Oslo's diversity.

CITY CENTRE

If he had to, Norway's King Harald could leave his palace on the hill every morning and walk down to the main station in Oslo in just 15 minutes. That's how

compact the city is. The centre basically comprises *Karl Johans gate* that runs from the Royal Palace to *Oslo sentralstasjon* – or Oslo S for short – and the streets leading off it.

Barely 2km (1¼mi) long, there are many things to see to the left and right of it as well as shops, bars, restaurants and parks. This is the heart of the capital, the political centre of the country, a place for entertainment and street art with magnificent buildings and a wide cultural spectrum. Everything can be reached on foot in just a few minutes and ● *Studenterlunden,* the park between the parliament building and the National Theatre that runs up one side, is a tempting place to relax and is a firm fixture for tours around Oslo city centre.

■1 AKER BRYGGE ★ ☼
(113 D2) (*ΩΩ G5*)

Aker Brygge is a popular entertainment district on Oslo Fjord. The brick buildings of this former shipyard are now home to shopping centre and boutiques, with bars and restaurants lining the quay. This is where you can go for a stroll and take in the fjord air, watch the ships go by, enjoy the view of Akershus Festning and perhaps have a drink in one of the restaurants along the promenade. On a beautiful summer's day, the people of Oslo come here in their thousands to soak up the sun and the sea – which can well mean that you won't find anywhere to sit in the bars and peace and quiet can only be found on a boat out on the fjord. From wherever you gaze at the water, you will always have the feeling that the maritime nation of Norway's heartbeat is never far away on Aker Brygge. If you fancy an un-disturbed breakfast down on the quayside, get up early, buy INSIDER TIP a bag of prawns from one of the fishing boats moored in front of the city hall at 8am and enjoy the view over the fjord. This classic Norwegian summer snack simply tastes best 'on the hoof'. *Tram 12: Aker Brygge*

■2 ASTRUP FEARNLEY MUSEET
(112 C3) (*ΩΩ F5*)

Since autumn 2012, the internationally renowned Astrup Fearnley Museum of Modern Art has been housed in two new buildings designed by the architect Renzo Piano at the tip of *Tjuvholmen* promontory. It has a sizeable collection of modern art by major Norwegian and international artists, including Andy Warhol and Damien Hirst. The holdings include the sculpture *Michael Jackson and Bubbles* by the American artist Jeff Koons. Information on new opening times and entrance fees can be found under *www.afmuseet.no | bus 21, 54: Aker Brygge*

MARCO POLO HIGHLIGHTS

★ **Aker Brygge**
Promenade with sea air and vibrant nightlife
→ p. 28

★ **Det Kongelige Slott**
The residence of the Norwegian royal family in the middle of the city
→ p. 31

★ **Nasjonalgalleriet**
The largest art collection in the country
→ p. 32

★ **Nobels Fredssenter**
Where all the Nobel Peace Prize winners are gathered → p. 33

★ **Akershus Festning og Slott**
The old fortress is a major landmark in Oslo high above the fjord
→ p. 35

★ **Oslo Rådhus**
Big, red and unmissable
→ p. 37

★ **Vigelandsparken**
World-famous sculptures that get people thinking → p. 41

★ **Munchmuseet**
With more than 20,000 works by the Expressionist painter → p. 45

★ **Operahuset**
Like a palace made of ice: Oslo's white Opera House is an eye-opener
→ p. 46

★ **Henie Onstad Kunstsenter**
Modern art in a wonderful setting on the fjord – thanks to an ice princess
→ p. 47

★ **Holmenkollen**
The gleaming new mecca for Nordic skiing fans
→ p. 48

3 IBSENMUSEET (113 D1) (*M G4*)

Henrik Ibsen (1828–1906), Norway's most famous playwright, is considered the founder of modern prose drama and one of the most important representatives of Realism. Even today he continues to be one of the most performed authors worldwide. Works such as *Peer Gynt*, *A Doll's House* and *The Wild Duck* have become classics. Despite the significant influence he had on world literature, Ibsen was never awarded the Nobel Prize. Ibsen lived near the palace from 1895 until his death in 1906. A literature museum has now been set up in this flat illustrating the life and work of the great poet. *Mid May–mid Sept Mon–Sun 11am–6pm, mid Sept–mid May Mon–Sun 11am–4pm, Thu 11am–6pm | guided tours on the hour | 85 NOK | Ibsengate 26 | www.norsk folkemuseum.no/ibsenmuseet | tram 19: Slottsparken*

4 KARL JOHANS GATE (113 E–F1) (*M H–J4*)

Every Norwegian knows Karl Johans gate – and virtually every travel guide calls the most famous road in the country an 'elegant boulevard'. This should however be taken with a pinch of salt: the pedestrian precinct from the station to the parliament building, Stortinget, is lined with less attractive shops and peopled by street vendors, beggars and drug addicts. It is only after the Grand Hotel that it opens out into a generously dimensioned boulevard where visitors can stroll through the park on the left with the splendid university building on the right, marvel at the façade of the National Theatre with the palace which dominates everything else further ahead. Karl Johans gate ends at the palace steps. The view from 🔆 *Slottsplassen* back down the street is truly breathtaking.

The country's most famous no-through-road: the Karl Johans gate on the National Day of Norway

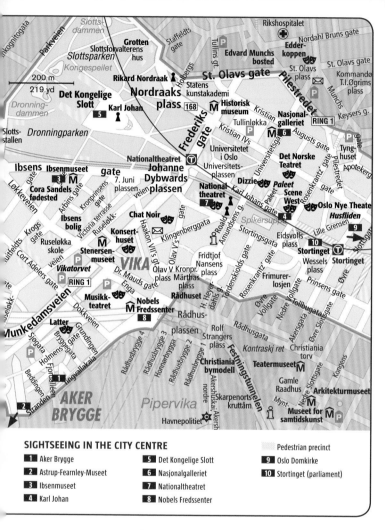

SIGHTSEEING IN THE CITY CENTRE

1 Aker Brygge
2 Astrup-Fearnley-Museet
3 Ibsenmuseet
4 Karl Johan

5 Det Kongelige Slott
6 Nasjonalgalleriet
7 Nationaltheatret
8 Nobels Fredssenter

▦ Pedestrian precinct
9 Oslo Domkirke
10 Stortinget (parliament)

5 DET KONGELIGE SLOTT ★
(107 E4–5) (*M G3*)

Since King Harald V gave the Skaugum estate to his son Haakon, he and Queen Sonja have been spending more time in Oslo – as the flag above the Royal Palace shows. The architect, Hans Ditlev Franciscus von Linstow, designed the building that was completed in 1848 in the Neoclassicist style. Following the dissolution of the Union with Sweden in 1905, it became the seat of the royal family when King Haakon VII moved in. The palace is surrounded by a large park that is open to

The National Theatre with the grand master Bjørnson himself

INSIDER **TIP** march up to the palace accompanied by a military band. *20 June–16 Aug guided tours of the palace in English every Mon–Thu, Sat noon, 2pm and 5pm, Fri/Sun 2pm, 2.20pm and 4pm (advance reservation strongly recommended) | 95 NOK | www.kongehuset.no | bus 30, 31, 32, 54, 70, 74, tram 13, 19: Nationaltheatret*

■6 NASJONALGALLERIET ★
(108 A5) (*∅ H3*)

The National Gallery, housing the most comprehensive collection of art in Norway, moved into its present premises on Universitetsgate in 1882. One of the gallery's focal points is Norwegian National Romanticism with works by Johan Christian Dahl, Adolph Tidemand, Hans Fredrik Gude and August Cappelen. The extensive collection of works by Edvard Munch is considered by many to be better than that in the Munch Museum. Works created after 1945 are not housed in the Nasjonalgalleriet but in the Museum of Contemporary Art. *Tue, Wed, Fri 10am–6pm, Thu 10am–7pm, Sat/Sun 11am–5pm | entrance fee 50 NOK, free on Sun | Universitetsgate 13 | www.nasjonalmuseet.no | tram 11, 17, 18: Tullinløkka*

■7 NATIONALTHEATRET
(113 E1) (*∅ H4*)

The architect Henrik Bull clad the National Theatre, that lies at the northwestern end of Studenterlunden Park, in brick and Norwegian granite. It first opened in 1899 with a performance of Henrik Ibsen's *An Enemy of the People* when the theatre was still in private ownership. The playwright himself sat in the front row at the première. Sculptures of two of Norway's leading writers, Bjørnstjerne Bjørnson and Henrik Ibsen, unveiled at the opening, stand in front of the building. *Johanne Dybwads plass 1 | bus 30, 31, 32, 54, 70, 74, tram 13, 19: Nationaltheatret*

the public. The section called *Dronningsparken*, the queens' park, to the side of the palace is particularly attractive. A statue of Dronning Maud (1869–1938), the first queen of independent Norway, marks the entrance. The statue of the Swedish King Karl Johan looks down the road that bears his name – the Karl Johans gate – from its vantage point in front of the palace.

On 17 May, the National Day of Norway, members of the royal family appear on the palace balcony and wave to the children's parade that passes by.

The King's Guard performs sentry duty outside the royal palace which can be visited on a guided tour in summer only. However, the ● Changing of the Guard takes place every day of the year at 1.30pm and is well worth watching. In summer, this is sometimes preceded by a

8 NOBELS FREDSSENTER ★
(113 E2) (📍 G4)

The Nobel Peace Prize was not to be awarded in Sweden but in Oslo. This was what the Swede Alfred Nobel specified in his will – exactly why has never been clearly explained. Perhaps Nobel did not trust Swedish politicians and considered the Norwegian parliament to be more progressive. Or else he wanted to express his admiration for the Norwegian writer Bjørnstjerne Bjørnson. Whatever the reason, it is certainly irritating for Sweden that the award of the most important Nobel prize which attracts the greatest media attention is not announced in Stockholm but by the Nobel Institute in Oslo every year at the beginning of October. The award ceremony itself is held in December in Oslo City Hall.

In the Nobel Peace Centre in the magnificently restored former West Station, visitors can find out more about Alfred Nobel, the Peace Prize and its recipients in a hands-on multi-media presentation. A separate display is always given to the most recent award winner. All other recipients are to be found in an 'electronic garden' whereas a 'magic book' provides in-depth information on Alfred Nobel's life. *Tue–Sun 10am–6pm | 80 NOK | Brynjulf Bulls plass 1 | Rådhusplassen | www.nobelsfredssenter.no | tram 12: Rådhusplassen*

9 OSLO DOMKIRKE
(114 B1–2) (📍 J4)

Oslo Cathedral, built in the Baroque style and inaugurated in 1697, was the setting of the wedding of Crown Prince Haakon Magnus and Mette-Marit in 2001. The principal Protestant church in the city is also the main church for the Oslo bishopric. The ceiling frescos by Hugo Lous Mohr cover an area of 16,000ft², the stained glass windows depicting the birth and life

RELAX & ENJOY

Huk **(110 B–C6)** (📍 *B8*) on Bygdøy is Oslo's best-known beach but, despite its popularity, swimmers and sunbathers don't get in each other's way. Barbecues, tables and benches have been installed near the beach (charcoal available at the little shop). Some visitors to Huk swap their bathing costumes for normal clothes to reach for culinary stars. The food served in the restaurant ● 🍴 *Hukodden* on the very edge of Huk is first rate and the panoramic view of the fjord bathed in the evening light is a perfect finish to a day in Oslo. *(Mon–Fri 5pm– 10pm, Sat/Sun from noon, depending on weather | tel. 67 10 99 70 | Strømsborgveien 46 |* *www.sult.no/hukodden | Moderate– Expensive). Bus 30 for example runs from the Nationaltheatret to Huk directly*

You don't need to be a guest at *Hotel Bristol* **(108 A5)** (📍 *H4*) to sample its organic 🍃 health packages. Therapies range from the aromatic and herbal to facial and full body treatments and are so good that you have to book in advance. A complete facial pampering session costs around 930 NOK; a half-day health and spa package incl. lunch approx. 2800 NOK *(Tue–Fri noon–7pm, Sat noon–6pm | reservations: tel. 22 33 55 55 | Rosenkrantzgate 3 | tram 11, 17, 18: Tinghuset).*

of Jesus were made by Emanuel Vigeland and installed in 1910. *Open 24 hours | free entrance | Karl Johans gate 11 | tram 11, 17, 18, bus 37: Stortorvet*

10 STORTINGET
(114 A1) *(🗺 H4)*

'All makt i denne salen' – 'all the power in these halls' chanted the liberal politician Johan Sverdrup in 1884 in Stortinget, the parliament building. Norwegian politicians had just voted in favour of parliamentarianism, having removed the power from the king of the union between Sweden and Norway, Oscar II, and transferred it to the Stortinget. It had been another king of Sweden, namely Oscar I, who had commissioned the building of Stortinget itself and it was in 1866 that Norwegian politicians first sat in the mellow yellow brick buildings on Karl Johans gate.

The two sculptures of lions designed by Christopher Borch that line the approach to the main entrance have given Stortinget its nickname *løve-bakken* (lions' hill). It was not Borch himself who actually carved the lions in granite, but a prisoner condemned to death who, as a sign of gratitude, was ultimately pardoned. *June–Aug guided tours in English Mon–Fri 10am, 11.30am and 1pm | free entrance | Karl Johans gate 22 | www.stortinget.no | T-bane 2, 3, 4, 5, 6: Stortinget*

KVADRA-TUREN

Kvadraturen is Oslo's 'old New Town'. Historical, architectural and artistic delights rub shoulders in this district between Akershus Fortress and what is today the city centre around Karl Johans gate.

In 1624, the old city of Oslo burned to the ground. King Christian IV had the new centre erected on the other side of Bjørvika Bay. Sheltered by the massive structure of Akershus Fortress, the new city was laid

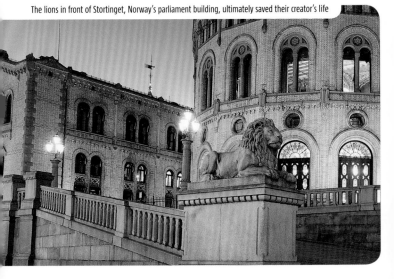

The lions in front of Stortinget, Norway's parliament building, ultimately saved their creator's life

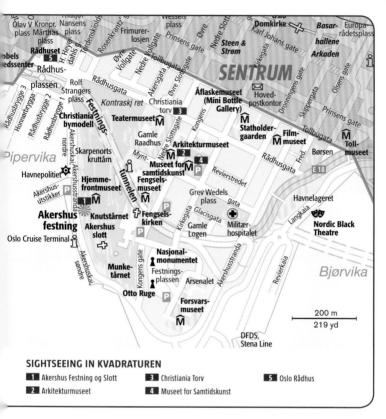

SIGHTSEEING IN KVADRATUREN

1 Akershus Festning og Slott   **3** Christiania Torv   **5** Oslo Rådhus

2 Arkitekturmuseet   **4** Museet for Samtidskunst

out on a strictly quadratic ground plan in the spirit of the Renaissance – hence its name *Kvadraturen* and the canyon-like streets with their sometimes rather bombastic architecture. Even though the centre has since shifted further westwards, Kvadraturen has remained Oslo's historical centre. The district is not only surprising due to its grid-like street plan but also to its many historical buildings. Rådhusgate still boasts several houses from the time Kvadraturen was first built; otherwise this compact district is dominated by impressive, 19th-century façades. During the day, Kvadraturen is an attractive area with a number of museums, whereas in the evening it is empty and forlorn.

1 AKERSHUS FESTNING OG SLOTT ★ (113 E3) (⑩ H5)

The fortress has survived nine serious sieges since the Middle Ages, with neither Sweden nor Denmark managing to take this bulwark on a promontory above Oslo Fjord. In medieval times Akershus was a royal fortress that Christian IV (1588–1648) turned into a Renaissance castle with massive fortifications. The ramparts and walls enclose an area some 350m by 100m. The northern end of the inner fortifica-

tions is formed by *Høymagasinet (historical model town display | June–Aug Tue–Sun 10am–3pm)*. At the southern end is *Munketårnet,* the monks' tower and former gunpowder store which marks the entrance. *Akershus Slott,* open in the summer, and *Hjemmefrontmuseet* lie

vaulted basement. *June–Aug Mon–Sat 10am–5pm, Sun 11am–5pm | 50 NOK | http://mil.no/culture-attractions/museums/norwayresistancemuseum*
A climb up the ⚜ rampart that rises behind the museum is an absolute must. The view of Oslo harbour and across to

Very fitting – the Ministry of Defence is housed in Akershus Fortress

within the fortifications. The *Christian IV Satal,* a hall used for special functions by the Norwegian government and a chapel are located in the south wing of the castle. The tombs of King Haakon VII and Olav V, as well as Queen Maud and Crown Princess Märtha are located in an extension to the mausoleum. *Castle and mausoleum May–Aug Mon–Sat 10am–4pm, Sun 12.30pm–4pm | guided tours in English Thu 1pm | 75 NOK | tram 12: Christiania Torv*
The *Hjemmefrontmuseum* that documents the Norwegian Resistance during World War II is between the castle and Høymagasinet. The exhibition is housed in the

Aker Brygge is magical at any time of the year but especially in summer with the whole of the inner fjord spread out below. Adjoining the fortress are the barracks, warehouses and stables. The carefully restored buildings are now used in part by the Norwegian Environment and Defence ministries as well as Oslo's mounted police. The *Forsvarsmuseet* is housed in the former armoury. The museum traces the military history of Norway from the Vikings to the present day. *May–Aug Mon–Fri 10am–5pm, Sat/Sun 11am–5pm, Sept–April Mon–Fri 11am–3pm, Sat/Sun 11am–4pm | free entrance | www.fmu.mil.no*

2 INSIDER TIP ARKITEKTURMUSEET
(113 F2) (*M H5*)

A cross-section of Norwegian architecture spanning three eras is accommodated in a building from 1830 that originally housed the Norges Bank. In 2008, the Norwegian architect Sverre Fehn used the space between the main building and the depot of 1911 to add a concrete and glass pavilion. The constrast of styles has since been the source of controversial debates among Norwegian architects and visitors alike. *Tue, Wed, Fri 11am–5pm, Thu 11am–7pm, Sat/Sun noon–5pm | entrance fee 50 NOK, free on Sun | Bankplassen 3 | www.nasjonalmuseet.no/en/venues/the_national_museum_architecture/ | bus 60: Bankplassen*

3 CHRISTIANIA TORV
(113 F2) (*M H5*)

It's rather like being in someone's private living room with pretty wallpaper. Low-rise historical and modern buildings frame the little picturesque square called Christiania torv that forms a striking contrast to the canyon-like streets in Kvadraturen. The hustle and bustle of the capital seems a long way away and it is indeed difficult to believe that this was once the very heart of Old Oslo where market tenders haggled with all their might and even executions took place.

Standing on the square looking east, two historical buildings stand out. The half-timbered *Rådmannsgården* on the left dates back to 1626. It is the oldest building in what was once Christiania and housed the military infirmary and the university library. A sculpture by the Norwegain artist Wenche Guldbrandsen – the hand of the city founder Christian IV – is in the middle of the square. A complete statue of the founding father of Kvadraturen is strangely enough (and historically incorrectly) on *Stortorvet,* Oslo's market square. To the right of Rådhusgate is the INSIDER TIP Gamle Rådhus, Christiania's first town hall from which its fortunes were managed between 1641 and 1733. Following a fire in 1996, the restaurant *Det Gamle Raadhus* was rebuilt as it had been before. The very cosy *Lauritz Ruus Bar* inside is a popular place for a hearty lunch *(Mon–Fri 11.30am–3pm | Moderate). Tram 12: Christiania torv*

4 MUSEET FOR SATMTIDSKUNST
(113 F3) (*M H5*)

In the former Central Bank, counters and safes have made way for contemporary art. Finished in marble and Norwegian granite, the building from 1907 now houses 4700 works by mostly Norwegian artists. The variety of temporary exhibitions is outstanding – ranging from traditional paintings to video installations, art films and experimental sound installations. Permanent exhibits include *Inner Room V* by the Norwgian artist Per Inge Bjørlo and *The Dustman* by the Russian Ilya Kabakov. *Tue, Wed, Fri 11am–5pm, Thu 11am–7pm, Sat/Sun noon–5pm | entrance fee 50 NOK, free on Sun | Bankplassen 4 | www.nasjonalmuseet.no | bus 60: Bankplassen*

5 OSLO RÅDHUS ★ (113 E2) (*M H4*)

In the 1920s and '30s, compulsory purchase orders were placed on houses in Oslo's harbour district Pipervika which were then demolished to make way for a monumental city hall, designed by the architects Arnstein Arneberg and Magnus Poulsson. Although the foundation stone was laid in 1931, it was not completed unitl 1950. Not everyone in Oslo is enamoured of the red brick building with its two massive, 60m (200ft)-high, square towers and refer to it – more or less affectionately – as *geitost*, the name of the typically Norwegian goats' cheese that is

sold in square lumps. Since traffic was forced underground a few years ago, the seat of Oslo's city council has become a visible landmark, acting as a gateway to the world. 49 bells in the clock tower make up northern Europe's largest *glockenspiel* and every Wed at 1pm a INSIDER TIP mini

The city hall is Oslo's massive gateway to the world

bell concert can be heard. The building houses a small art museum in rooms decorated by Henrik Sørensen and Alf Rolfsen. Other artists who lent a helping hand include Per Krogh, Dyre Vaa and Edvard Munch (The Munch Room). Once a year the city hall becomes the focus of world attention when the Nobel Peace

Prize is awarded in the Great Hall on 10 Dec. *Daily 9am–6pm, guided tours daily 10am, noon, 2pm | free entrance | Rådhusplassen 1 | tram 12: Rådhusplassen*

FROGNER

The area between the palace and Frogner Park has always been for the more affluent. The roads around Majorstuen underground station are lined with late 19th and early 20th-century properties. Many town villas that lie slightly back from the road now house embassies and consulates. Frogner has in fact always been trendy although it may seem rather staid.

It is known for its green spaces with plenty of room for children and its neighbourly togetherness. Splendid villas surrounded by lovely gardens as well as blocks of flats – called 'city courtyards' – on other roads, some with bay windows, others without, are a delight for those interested in architecture. The most famous and beautiful public parks in the city are in Frogner, the loveliest part of which is between Frognerveien and Gyldenløves gate. Both roads lead to Frogner Park.

■1■ FROGNERPARKEN ●
(106 A–B 1–2) (*ﬂ D–E 1–2*)

This jewel among Oslo's parks is also the most visited tourist attraction in the capital. As the world famous Vigeland Sculpture Park (see Vigelandsparken) is located at the southern tip of the park and most visitors want to have a few pictures of the monumental sculptures, they have little time for a longer walk through the exceptionally beautiful and romantic landscaped park. 3000 trees, including exotic specimens such as magnolias, maidenhair or ginkgo trees and giant redwoods line the paths. Norway's largest rose gar-

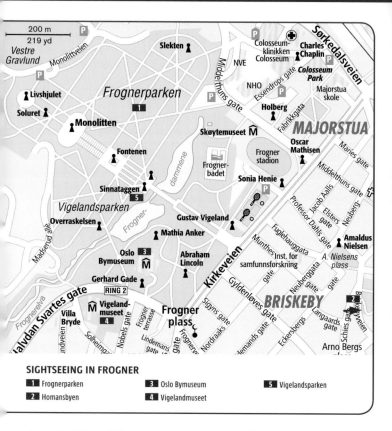

SIGHTSEEING IN FROGNER

1 Frognerparken
2 Homansbyen
3 Oslo Bymuseum
4 Vigelandmuseet
5 Vigelandsparken

den, with 150 varieties and around 14,000 different plants, also forms part of Frogner Park.

The people of Oslo descend on Frogner Park at the weekend in particular, picnic basket in hand, and stay there until late in the evening. This also has something to do with long-standing traditions connected with the swimming pool and stadium in the park. Back in 1901 an ice rink was built where many championships were held up until the 1930s. The Norwegian football team played its first international match in 1910 against Sweden in *Frogner stadion*. The outdoor pool *Frognerbadet*

on the northern edge of the park was opened in the 1950s and is still as popular as ever *(Mon–Fri 7am–7.30pm, Sat/Sun 10am–6pm | 80 NOK)*. On warm summer days, up to 4000 seek out the 7½-acre park – at the annual *Norwegian Wood* rock festival there are at least five times this number. *Open 24 hours all year round | bus 20, tram 12: Vigelandsparken or Frogner stadion, T-bane: Majorstuen*

2 INSIDER TIP HOMANSBYEN
(107 E3) (*Ø G2*)

In the second half of the 19th century, northern Europe's first estate of purpose-

built houses for the open market was erected between Uranienborgveien in the south and Pilestredet in the north. Unfortunately, the impression of the estate as a whole has been spoiled by the volume of traffic and new buildings in the area. However, if you look closely, you can easily see the magnificent ornamental details. Inspired by English urban colonies, the Homan brothers built large properties from 1858 onwards along *Oscars gate*, *Josefines gate* and *Gustavs gate*, aimed at attracting Oslo's expanding number of civil servants. From the very outset, there were to be no factories, small businesses or restaurants here. This was an area people could withdraw to and lead private lives. Among the most attractive examples of elaborate architectural detailing are *Josefines gate 13*, built in 1860 in the Neo-Gothic French château style with towers and an elaborately decorated roof façade, and *Uranienborgslott,* a villa in the Neo-Renaissance style with a tower and cupola, located on an elevated site to the southwest of Homansbyen. Unfortunately these can only be viewed from the road. *Tram 11: Homansbyen*

■3 OSLO BYMUSEUM
(106 B2–3) (*⅏ E2*)

This wonderful manor house in the Danish style which was given a mock Tudor makeover at the end of the 18th century – something definitely not typically Norwegian – is beautifully located in a quiet corner of Frogner Park. It now houses the municipal museum which focuses on Oslo's history from the Middle Ages to the present day. The most striking room on the first floor of the main building is the ballroom of the chamberlain Bernt Anker that was added during extensive remodelling in the 1790s. The walls in the upper rooms are decorated with 19th-century Oslo landscape paintings. The Oslo Theatre Museum is also now housed in the municipal museum. *Tue–Sun 11am–5pm | free entrance | Frognerveien 67 | www.oslomuseum.no | bus 20, tram 12: Frogner plass*

■4 VIGELANDMUSEET
(106 A3) (*⅏ D2*)

While Vigeland Park contains many works of art, it is Vigeland Museum that was the place of work. Gustav Vigeland used the rooms in the Neo-Classicist villa that is

just a five-minute walk from the park as his studio. He lived and worked here from 1924–43 and left some 1600 sculptures, 12,000 drawings and 300 woodcuts for posterity. The urn with the artist's ashes is kept in the museum tower. 3 of a total of 14 rooms are reserved for temporary exhibitions and for works by other artists. *June–Aug Tue–Sun 10am–5pm, Sept–May noon–4pm | April–Sept 50 NOK, Oct–March free entrance | Nobelsgate 32 | www. vigeland.museum.no | bus 20, tram 12: Frogner plass*

up into 5 groups: the Main Gate, the Bridge with children's playground where the famous sculpture *Sinnataggen* (Angry Boy) can be found, the Fountain, the raised plateau with the Monolith and the Wheel of Life. The significance of the 17m (56ft)-high Monolith in particular, which comprises 121 figures carved out of one stone, is still a source of mystery among art historians. Does it represent the aspiration for higher things, the vision of a resurrection or is it merely an expression of the common bond between man? Vigeland

Stonemasons took 14 years to complete Gustav Vigeland's *Monolith*

⑤ VIGELANDSPARKEN ★ ●
(106 A–B 1–2) (ﾛ D–E 1–2)

The 212 sculptures made of bronze, granite and wrought iron by the sculptor Gustav Vigeland (1869–1943) attract more than 1 million visitors every year. Northern Europe's best-known sculpture collection was laid out on a 850m-long axis in Frogner Park to plans drawn up by the artist himself. Vigeland divided his works

designed this work of art in 1924–25. It took 3 stonemasons a total of 14 years to complete it.

If you feel like a pleasant stroll around Vigeland Park on a summer's evening, go up to the Monolith and watch the INSIDER TIP sunset – but look east instead! The view takes in the houses on the slopes to the east of the city which reflect the deep red evening light, casting it onto the

roofs of the capital. The spectacle behind your back is not that much less spectacular either! The Holmenkollen ski jump lies in the shadow of the setting sun. An unforgettably beautiful end to a day's holiday in Oslo. *Open 24 hours all year | free entrance | www.vigeland.museum.no | tram 12: Vigelandsparken or Frogner stadion, T-bane 1–6: Majorstuen*

THE EAST

Gamlebyen, the Old Town, is where Oslo began. It was only after 1624, following the building of the Kvadraturen district, that the city's centre shifted from the east to the west. The area to the east of Akerselva remained an industrial, working-class district, forming the capital's 'back yard', with major social problems.

All this has changed over the past few years. Oslo's east has gained in appeal and its modern architecture has attracted young people in particular. Districts such as Grünerløkka have shed their mustiness and are now regarded as trendy, bursting with vitality, a high standard of living and culture.

Oslo's proud new addition – the Opera House – has quite consciously been place in Bjørvika Bay in the east rather than in the gentrified west. Once the traffic has been banned into tunnels and under the fjord, then the white Opera House will form a focal point for urban redevelopment in the east.

■■ GAMLEBYEN
(115 E3–4) (*Ⅲ L5–6*)

The road up to *Gamlebyen* – the Old Town and the heart of historical Oslo – is remi-

The new Opera House has revitalised the east of the city

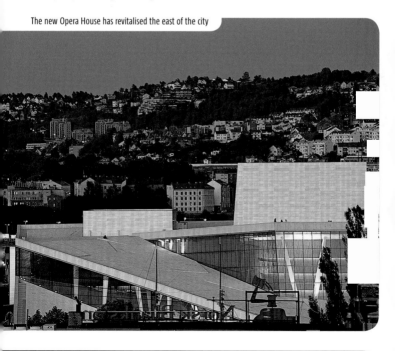

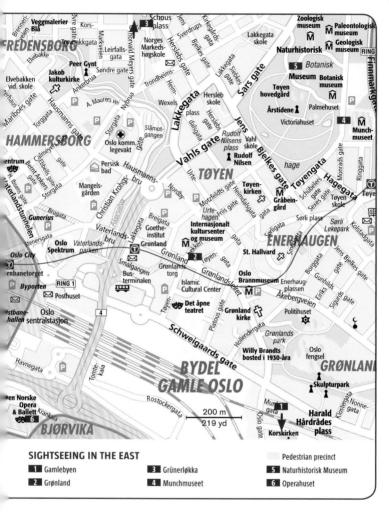

SIGHTSEEING IN THE EAST

1 Gamlebyen
2 Grønland
3 Grünerløkka
4 Munchmuseet

Pedestrian precinct
5 Naturhistorisk Museum
6 Operahuset

niscent of little coastal towns in Italy. Blocks of flats up to five storeys high have left their mark on this district but it is also characterised by its spacious feel and the many historical buildings. Lots of young people have chosen to live here and many immigrants have also settled in Gamlebyen. The *Sultan Grill* and the traditional restaurant *Oslo Spiseforetning* are located side by side – a positive expression of the district's multicultural bond.

1000 years ago, up until the great fire of 1624, Gamlebyen was Oslo. It lay between Bjørvika Bay and Grønland, climbing a little way up Ekeberg. Although medieval Oslo only stretched over a length of 600m

and had just 3000 inhabitants, it was an important centre of power. It was here that goods were traded and it was the seat of kings and bishops with six church-

A street scene in Grønland

es and three monasteries. The remains of the former religious and secular centre of power can still be seen to this day. In **INSIDER TIP** *Minneparken*, the ruins of St Hallvard's Cathedral, St Olav's Monastery and St Clemens' Church can be seen next to the present bishop's see on St Halvards plass 3 *(tram 18, 19, bus 70: St Halvards plass)*. The cathedral was built around 1100 in the Romanesque style and was Norway's largest church after Nidarosdomem in Trondheim. The bishopric seat was built on the ruins of St Olav's Monastery. A short walk towards the fjord will take you to *Middelalderparken*, hemmed in between railway tracks and the motorway. This was once a centre of power ruled by noblemen and is now the site of the ruins of St Mary's, the church and burial place of medieval kings. The

kings' fort with an impressive great hall was also located here on the fjord. *Vannspeilet,* the small artificial lake, marks the position of the fjord shoreline in the Middle Ages.

② GRØNLAND
(115 D1–2) (*ш K–L4*)

A young woman in a chador and a punk push their prams down the pavement side by side, chatting away to each other. Behind them, the minarets of a mosque can be seen. Grønland, slightly hidden behind Oslo S – the central station – and bordered by Grünerløkka to the north and Gamlebyen to the south, is Oslo's cultural melting pot. This is where sober Scandinavian culture comes face to face with a bundle of foreign influences. During the 1960s, a lot of immigrants from Pakistan in particular settled here, resulting in the district's nickname 'Little Karachi'. Exotic-looking shops, foreign aromas, unknown languages – Grønland is home to the whole world. And yet there are also lots of typically Norwegian things here too, such as *Asylet* opposite Grønland torg. Built in 1740 as a merchant's house, it has subsequently been used as a court and hospital, a children's and old people's home. It now houses a traditional restaurant. You won't exactly be pressed into buying a carpet in the *bazaar* (corner of Grønlandleiret/Tøyenbekken), but you will find the typically Norwegian *Vinmonopolet* rubbing shoulders with the *Thai House* in this Oriental-like shopping centre. In Grønland you can really experience the exciting sybiosis of cultures. *T-bane 2, 3, 4, 5, 6: Grønland*

③ GRÜNERLØKKA
(109 D2–4) (*ш K2–3*)

Grünerløkka is often referred to as the 'best district' in the east. When the city boundary was extended in 1858, for fire-

safety reasons brick houses were built to the east of the little Akerselva river, marking an end to the era of wooden buildings. The rate at which the district grew was so fast that Grünerløkka at that time was called 'Ny York'.

In the 1960s and '70s, the four and five-storey blocks of flats arranged around an inner courtyard, typical of Grünerløkka, had become so run down that the whole

interesting in Grünerløkka apart from the little corner cafés. The shops have everything from Norwegian designer clothes and modern ceramics to exotic vegetables. Anyone strolling down Thorvald Meyers gate, Grünerløkka's main thoroughfare on a summer's day *(tram 11, 12, 13: Olaf Ryes plass),* can soak up an atmosphere that can well be compared to the hustle and bustle on Karl Johans gate.

Thanks to squatters, Grünerløkka was saved from being knocked down

district was to have been demolished and rebuilt in a more modern style. Squatters prevented this and more and more young people and artists moved to Grünerløkka. The former working-class area is a vibrant centre once again since it became fashionable to live in a multicultural district surrounded by artists and immigrants. The few industrial workers that Oslo has left continue to live here too. There's lots going on here: open-air concerts, exhibitions and documentary film sessions – culture vultures can always find something

◼ MUNCHMUSEET ★
(109 F5) *(∅ M3)*

One of the most famous Norwegians of all time is the artist Edvard Munch (1863–1944). Munch, who also left a huge number of graphic works, is considered one of the major precursors of Expressionism. The museum (1963) in Tøyen, between Grünerløkka and Gamlebyen, houses the most extensive collection of his works. Munch bequeathed 1100 paintings, 15,500 graphic works and 4700 drawings to the City of Oslo.

The comprehensive exhibition provides an excellent insight into the life and work of the Norwegian artist whose world-famous paintings *The Scream* and *Girls on a Bridge* are of incalculable value.

What big eyes you have Ida! So this is what our ancestors once looked like

June–Aug Mon–Fri 10am–9pm, Sat 11am–5pm, Sun 11am–9pm, otherwise Tue–Thu 10am–9pm, Fri 10am–4pm, Sat 11am–5pm, Sun 11am–9pm | 95 NOK in summer, otherwise free | Tøyengata 53 | www.munch.museum.no | T-bane 1–6: Tøyen

⑤ NATURHISTORISK MUSEUM
(109 E–F4) (*ØØ L3*)

INSIDER TIP *Ida's* home is the museum's fossil department. Proven as the first primate in history, she lived more than 47 million years ago. The astonishingly complete fossil was found south of Frankfurt in Germany and was acquired by the Oslo museum in 2007. In May 2009 the results of analyses carried out by the Norwegian palaeontologist Jörn Hurum were presented: Ida is the 'missing link' in evolution between the animal kingdom and human beings.

The museum's *botanical garden* is a green oasis. The *scented garden* with some 90 different plants is particularly lovely (laid out for the visually impaired and wheelchair users). Norway's mountain flora can be admired in the *fjellhagen,* the Alpine garden. Some 1400 different plants thrive in a miniature mountain landscape with streams and waterfalls. *Museum Tue–Sun 11am–4pm, Botanical Garden mid March–Sept Mon–Fri 7am–9pm, Sat/Sun 10am–9pm, Oct–mid March Mon–Fri 7am–5pm, Sat/Sun 10am–5pm | entrance fee Museum 50 NOK | Satrsgate 1 | near the Munch museum | T-bane 1–6: Tøyen, bus 60: Tøyen kirken*

⑥ OPERAHUSET ★
(114 B–C3) (*ØØ J–K5*)

The Opera House, located right on Bjørvika Bay and opened in 2008, is Oslo's pride and joy. The idea dreamt up by the architectural practice Snøhetta was to create a building like an iceberg rising out of Oslo Fjord.

Whether of ice or marble – the extremely unconventional shape of the Opera House leaves nobody cold. Snøhetta created a monument to design and a landmark of international repute in a more-or-less disused corner of Oslo harbour. And it is not only specialists who compare the

building to Sydney's famous opera house and are full of praise for the cubist shape and fascinating interplay of white stone and lots of glass.

The new building is intended to be an opera house which you can get your hands on – literally. The ☀ marble roof that slopes down to the water is made for people to walk on and, if you climb up it, you'll be rewarded with a lovely view of Oslo and the harbour area. The people of Oslo have welcomed their new opera house with open arms and discovered that you can even ● INSIDER TIP picnic on the roof. *Foyer Mon–Fri 10am–11pm, Sat 11am–11pm, Sun noon–10pm, guided tours in English daily 2pm, ticket office Mon–Fri 9am–8pm, Sat 11am–6pm, Sun noon–6pm | 5 mins. on foot from Oslo S via the pedestrian bridge | www.operaen.no*

IN OTHER DISTRICTS

ST HANSHAUGEN
(108 A–B 1–2) (*m H–J 1–2*)
To the northwest of Frogner, behind the famous Bislett sports stadium, lies the district of St Hanshaugen where, once again, a park forms the central feature. From 1850 onwards, St Hanshaugen Park was laid out in the style of an English landscape garden, reaching its present shape in 1910. The *tårnhuset*, a 14m (46ft)-high tower in the Neo-Renaissance style at the ☀ highest point in the park, forms a central feature from where you have one of the best views of the city and fjord.

St Hanshaugen Park's heyday started in 1890. The park and restaurant were so popular in summer that, in the 1930s, the gardener complained that the whole park stank of sweat. Few concerts are now held in the park, but the *midsummer night's festival* in the park is an absolute highlight, not only for those living in this district. *Bus 21, 37, 46: St. Hanshaugen*

FURTHER AFIELD

INSIDER TIP EMANUEL VIGELAND MUSEUM (0) (*m 0*)
Emanuel Vigeland (1875–1948), the younger brother of the better-known Gustav Vigeland, had a museum built in 1926 for his own sculptures and paintings. In the early 1940s, the artist, who was strongly influenced by the Italian Renaissance, transformed the museum into a mausoleum: *Tomba Emmanuelle* (Emanuels' Tomb). All windows were blocked up and he named the fresco that covers the walls and ceiling *Vita*. Taking the Creation and the Fall of Man at motifs, Emanuel Vigeland painted hundreds of naked figures of men and women symbolising eroticism and sexual drive. The effect is intensified by the lack of light in the mausoleum, with the dramaturgy of the work of art unfolding only gradually – quite an experience! *15 May–15 Sept only Sun noon–5pm, 16 Sept–14 May Sun noon–4pm | entrance fee 40 NOK | Grimelundsveien 8 | www.emanuelvigeland.museum. no | T-bane 1: Slemdal*

HENIE ONSTAD KUNSTSENTER ★ (0) (*m 0*)
Art on the fjord – in the Henie Onstad Art Centre some 15km (9½mi) west of Oslo, impressive architecture, a fjord landscape and a little bit of Hollywood fuse with exceptional works of modern European art. It owes its name to the Norwegian figure skater and Hollywood star in the 1920s and '30s, Sonja Henie. The art col-

The gigantic new ski jump at Holmenkollen

lection bequest – mainly works by modern French artists – amassed by Henie and her husband, the shipowner Niels Onstad, form the basis of the art centre.

The building, designed by the two Norwegians Jon Eikvar and Sven Erik Engebretsen, opens up like a fan towards the fjord, stretching out from the Høvikodden promontory. The art museum, comprising 110 works from the Henie Collection, was opened in 1968. The graves of Henie and her husband are on the hill above the centre. Works from the collection and temporary exhibitions of works by important Norwegian and international artists are held in the 32,500ft² exhibition area. Henry Moore's *Knife Edge* is one of the principal works in the sculpture park. A short walk can be recommended that takes you from the park through the woods to the banks of the fjord, from where you can follow the shoreline heading towards Oslo as far as the ⚜ Veritas building. From there you have a lovely view of Fornebu Peninsula where Olso airport was once located. *Tue–Fri 11am–7pm, Sat/Sun 11am–5pm | entrance fee 80 NOK, Wed free | www.hok. no | bus 151 from Oslo central bus station every 15 min., travel time approx. 25 mins. Høvikodden*

HOLMENKOLLEN ⭐ ● ⚜
(116 B5) (*Ⓜ 0*)

The Nordic World Ski Championships in spring 2011 was the first major international event to be held at the new ski jump. The futuristically designed and generously proportioned jump looks like a huge soup ladle. It offers wonderful views over Oslo as can well be imagined even at the base. At the 2011 championships, attended by some 1.2 million people, the most famous of all ski jumps in the world once again became a skiing mecca. The ⚜ platform on the tower provides a spectacular view over Oslo, the fjord and Marka *(ski museum and jump June–Aug daily 9am–8pm, May/Sept 10am–5pm, otherwise 10am–4pm | entrance fee 100 NOK for the museum and tower)*. Apart from the ski museum where the Øvrebø ski from the 16th century is on display, among other things, the ski simulator, the

MARKA (0) (*⌘ 0*)

If you ask the people of Oslo what the most beautiful place in their city is, the spontaneous answer is often 'Marka'! Northern Europe's largest recreation area near a city is part of Oslo's identity. Surrounding the city basin like a huge green crown, the waymarked walks through the endless expanse of forest are perfect for hikes in summer and for cross-country skiing on well-maintained tracks in winter. The network of cross-country tracks through the Marka alone extends to 2600km (1620mi). If you would like to spend several days here, there are a number of lodges run by the Norwegian hiking club, DNT, where you can book a bunk bed and yet still be within the Oslo municipal area. Most lodges are run as guesthouses and offer hot meals and a hearty hiker's breakfast. Hiking maps are available in bookshops. More detailed information on the lodges is available on the DNT website *(www.turistforeningen. no)*. The best starting points for tours through the forests in Marka are *Holmenkollen* and *Frognerseter*. If you just want to go for a jog or a short walk with the children, you can also start from either of these stops on T-bane line 1 and simply follow the signs.

glazed lift up the outer wall of the jump centre, the small café and the summer training sessions held here are further reasons for spending a few hours at Holmenkollen. Don't miss out on a walk to ☀ INSIDER TIP *Holmenkollen kapell*. The dark-stained wooden chapel is used by the royal family on special occasions. The view over Oslo and the forests of Nordmarka is quite beautiful. *T-bane 1: Holmenkollen*

A PASSION FOR SPORT

It's not money but sport and the fun factor that count at the football event with the greatest number of participants in the world. Some 30,000 boys and girls aged 10–19 from 50 different nations and from all continents gather at the beginning of August on the *Ekebergsletta* sports fields to the east of the city to battle it out for the *Norway5Cup (www. norwaycup.no)*. Quite a sight!

Norway is the birthplace of skiing and the *Holmenkollen* ski arena is a mecca for all cross-country skiers, biathletes and ski jumpers. Anyone in Oslo between February and March should check out *www.holmenkollen.com* to see if a local championship or even a World Cup event is taking place, reserve a ticket and soak up the atmosphere at Holmenkollen at least once in a lifetime.

FOOD & DRINK

One person who is really in the know denies that there is such a thing as traditional Oslo cooking. Eyvind Hellstrøm, Norway's first but – for some time now – not the only winner of the world cookery championship *Bocuse d'Or*, is the country's most famous chef and has unsuccessfully been trying to find the genuine 'Oslo cuisine'. Hellstrøm is now convinced that there is no such thing. But like all visitors to Oslo, he can also rest assured that an excellent international scene now exists instead.

Naturally, grandma's old recipes, such as *kjøttkaker* (meat balls) in brown sauce or *flesk og duppe,* fried bacon in white sauce

with potatoes, taste delicious. These are as close as you'll come to a traditional 'Oslo cuisine' – filling and not too expensive. Of course, one fish dish in particular shouldn't be left out: *fersk torsk* – fresh cod – that really does taste best in those months with an 'r' in their name and less so in summer.

Nevertheless there is a good range of choice and interesting dishes on Oslo's menus that can largely be attributed to the wide range of international specialities. That also means that you can eat more cheaply and well in expensive Norway. Asian food is predominant, especially Indian and Pakistani fare. The

Photo: Ekeberg-Restauranten with a view of Oslo Fjord

From grandma's cookery book or *Bocuse d'Or*? Oslo boasts good home cooking and gourmet cuisine but not much in between

next kebab stand and hot dog booth are never far away either. Norwegian snackbars or *gatekjøkken*, offering *pølse* (sausages) either boiled or grilled, can also be found on every street corner. The Norwegians are fast becoming world champions in easy-to-eat fast food. Gourmets can be consoled that, at the other end of the scale, there is enough choice as well.

A strange anomaly in Norway is that *middag* is not eaten at midday as the name would imply, but in the evening. Restaurants start to fill up from 7pm onwards but open their doors at 5pm. The people of Oslo have lunch between 11.30am and 2pm and like to go to restaurants too. Many places have lunch menus with smaller portions at much cheaper prices. Beer and wine are expensive and it is quite

The excellent wines at Dr. Kneipp's Vinbar are available even without a prescription

normal just to order *vann* (tap water) with your meal. You usually pay by credit card in restaurants, cafés and bars and very seldom in cash.

Most places that call themselves 'cafés' also have hot meals and do not necessarily have cakes. These can be found in a *konditori*. The prices in cafés are also not much different from in restaurants.

CAFÉS

INSIDERTIP GODT BRØD ☺
(109 D3) *(ⓜ K2)*

The bakery is on view to all and customers, young and old, adore the fresh bread and *boller* – buns of all sorts. Everything is organic and that little bit more expensive, but it is absolutely delicious. Open from 6am. *Thorvald Meyersgate 49 | tram 11, 12, 13: Olav Ryes plass; branches: Theresegate 33* **(107 F1)** *(ⓜ H1)* and *Nydalen Allé 1* **(105 D3)** *(ⓜ O)*

KAFFEEBRENNERIET

Coffee shops are shooting up like mushrooms everywhere in Oslo. *Kaffeebrenneriet* now has some 20 branches in the city and has surprisingly cheap prices and very good coffee. The pastries & co. they serve are made in their own bakery. There are two branches in the centre. *Closed Sun | Storgata 2* **(108 B6)** *(ⓜ J4)* | *Akersgata 45* **(108 A5)** *(ⓜ J4)*

PASCAL KONDITORI (107 E5) *(ⓜ G4)*

The confectioner Pascal Dupuy in Henrik Ibsens gate opposite the palace has won several awards for his delicious cakes and snacks. The former US president Bill Clinton stopped by here too. *Henrik Ibsens gate 36 | tram 13, 19: Slottsparken*

VALKYRIEN TE & KAFFE ●
(106 C1) *(ⓜ F1)*

Anyone strolling around the west of the city near Frogner Park should call in here

for a cup of tea or coffee where you will be met with a friendly smile and knowledgeable staff as well as the waft of wonderful beverages from all over the world. There's not much room but that will give you time to have a look around and buy something to take back home. *Kirkeveien 59 | tram 11, 12, 19: Majorstuen*

WAYNE'S COFFEE
(107 D5) *(⫟ F4)*

There are four branches of this coffee shop in Oslo which are considered second to none by coffee fans. You can also enjoy a cup outside at the branch on Solli plass to the southwest of the royal park. *Henrik Ibsens gate 90 | tram 12, 13, bus 30, 31: Solli plass*

RESTAURANTS: EXPENSIVE

EKEBERG-RESTAURANTEN ★ ☆
(115 D5) *(⫟ K–L7)*

Continental cuisine above Oslo Fjord with a wonderful view. Wide selection also at lunchtime. *Kongsveien 15 | tel. 23 24 23 00 | www.ekebergrestauranten.com | tram 18, 19: Sjømannsskolen*

GREFSENKOLLEN ☆
(0) *(⫟ 0)*

Superlative cuisine in the most beautiful hilly countryside imaginable with lovely views, a musk ox over the mantelpiece and an open kitchen. *Closed Mon | Grefsenkollveien 100 | tel. 22 79 70 60 | bus 56: Trollveiskrysset, 15 mins. walk.*

LOFOTEN (113 D3) *(⫟ G5)*

An exclusive fish restaurant suitably located on the quayside on Aker Brygge. Fresh fish and seafood from Norwegian fishing grounds. Traditionally served but never uninspiring. *Stranden 75 | tel. 22 83 08 08 | www.lofoten-fiskerestaurant.no | tram 12: Aker Brygge*

MARKVEIEN MAT & VINHUS
(108 C4) *(⫟ K3)*

Long before Grünerløkka was 'in', a mixture of French and Norwegian fare was served here. Exclusive wines and certain dishes from the main menu can be ordered more cheaply in the adjoining INSIDER TIP ▶ *Dr. Kneipp's Vinbar*. *Closed Sun | Torvbakkgata 12, entrance Markveien | tel. 22 37 22 97 | tram 11, 12, 13: Nybrua*

STATHOLDERENS MAT & VINKJELLER (114 A2) *(⫟ J5)*

Bent Stiansen knows how to create a feast for the senses. He has expanded his famous

MARCO POLO HIGHLIGHTS

⭐ **Ekeberg-Restauranten**
Which is better, the view or the food. Both are difficult to beat → p. 53

⭐ **Lofotstua**
Excellent, fresh fish – served in a setting like a fisherman's home → p. 55

⭐ **Le Canard**
Choice Norwegian ingredients meet the French culinary art and good wine → p. 54

⭐ **Restaurant Oscarsgate**
Small, excellent and unpretentious → p. 54

⭐ **Palace Grill**
No menu or wine list here – but a lot of charm and a relaxed atmosphere instead → p. 55

⭐ **Lorry**
The classic Oslo pub with famous faces and plain fare → p. 57

Statholdergaarden with a new restaurant in the cellar. Culinary delights from around the world are served in the vaulted room from the 17th century. Duck, cod, venison and shellfish – Norway meets Asia, France and North Africa. Be prepared for quite an experience! *Closed Sun/Mon | Rådhusgaten 11 | tel. 22 41 88 00 | www.statholdergaarden.no | tram 10, 12, 13, 15, 17: Posthuset*

RESTAURANTS: MODERATE

BRASSERIE 45 (113 E1) (*ØØ H4*)

Although this restaurant is opposite the National Theatre it's not that easy to find, as it is located on the first floor of the building in which the Norwegian Christian Democratic Party has its offices. The décor is somewhat understated but the staff make up for this with very good service. The menu always has four exciting 3-course meals; the mixture of Asian and French cuisine is certainly to be recommended. *Mon–Thu 3pm–11pm, Fri/Sat 2pm–midnight, Sun 2pm–10pm | Stortingsgaten 20, entrance Roald Amundsens gate | www.brasserie45.no | bus 30, 31, 32, 54, 70, 74, tram 13, 19: Nationaltheatret*

KAFFISTOVA (114 A1) (*ØØ H4*)

Kaffistova in Hotel Bondeheimen offers typically Norwegian fare that includes *raspeballer* (dumplings from the west

GOURMET RESTAURANTS

Le Canard ★ (106 C4) (*ØØ F3*)

Listed in the Guide Michelin, with the best wine list in Oslo and impeccable service. Exclusive Norwegian and French ingredients are perfectly balanced in regal surroundings in this internationally famous restaurant. Main course from £33 (52US$). *Mon–Sat from 6pm | President Harbitz gate 4 | tel. 22 54 34 00 | www.lecanard.no | tram 19: Briskeby*

Feinschmecker (106 B4) (*ØØ E3*)

This restaurant in the Frogner district is modest in style with a classical cuisine. The head chef in Feinschmecker – a silver-medal winner of the international *Bocuse d'Or* competition – is of top European standard. One speciality: Arctic char. Main course from £33 (52US$). *Mon–Sat from 5pm | Balchens gate 5 | tel. 22 12 93 80 | www.feinschmecker.no | bus 30, 31: Frogner kirke*

Restaurant Oscarsgate ★ (107 F3) (*ØØ G2*)

Imaginative food of extremely high standard has earned this restaurant a Michelin star. Despite the intimate atmosphere in this small restaurant there is nothing snobby about the place. But that doesn't make it any cheaper. An 8-course meal costs £110 (170US$). *Tue–Sat from 6pm | Pilestredet 63 | tel. 22 46 59 06 | www.restaurantoscarsgate.no | tram 17, 18: Dalsbergstien*

Statholdergaarden (114 A2) (*ØØ J5*)

Exclusive restaurant in the 18th-century style with the very best cuisine. The Michelin star chef Bent Stiansen conjures up both classical and imaginative dishes using season Norwegian produce. Main course from £32 (50US$). *Mon–Sat from 6pm | Rådhusgata 11 | tel. 22 41 88 00 | www.statholdergaarden.no | tram 10, 12, 13, 15, 17: Posthuset*

coast) and *boknafisk,* traditionally smoke-dried stockfish. *Rosenkrantz gate 8 | tel. 61 17 15 29 | tram 11, 17, 18: Stortorvet*

LOFOTSTUA ⭐
(106 C1–2) (*ɯ F1*)
Eat fish at least once in proper Norwegian style – without any frills and with the refreshing added bonus of the northern Norwegians' unhurried way of life. *Mon–Fri from 3pm | Kirkeveien 40 | tel. 22 46 93 96 | bus 20, tram 11, 12, 19, T-bane 1–6: Majorstuen*

INSIDER TIP OSLO SPISEFORRETNING
(115 E3) (*ɯ L5*)
Traditional Norwegian recipes are interpreted in a modern way in this cosy restaurant. Extensive wine list. *Tue–Sat from 4pm | Oslo gate 15 | tel. 22 62 62 10 | bus 34, 45, 46, 70, tram 18, 19: St. Halvards plass/Dyvekes Bro*

PALACE GRILL ⭐ ☘
(107 D5) (*ɯ F4*)
The best place in Oslo for those who like things a bit more informal. There is neither a menu nor a wine list, but just a 10-course meal of the day that can be happily adapted to diners' wishes and is prepared using the best ingredients only. Seats 23, no reservations possible – just knock on the door and give it a try! Even the price is surprisingly low. *Mon–Sat from 5pm | Solli gata 2 | tel. 23 13 11 40 | tram 12, 13, bus 30, 31: Solli plass*

SULT (109 D2) (*ɯ K1*)
Sult means 'hunger' and is the title of Knut Hamsun's best-known novel. In the restaurant of the same name, creative cooks staunch the hunger of guests with fish in particular that is prepared in a contemporary and sometimes surprising manner. *Mon–Fri from 4pm, Sat/Sun from noon | Thorvald Meyers gate 26 B |*

Palace Grill: 23 seats, 10 courses, no menu

tel. 67 10 99 70 | tram 11, 12, 13, bus 30: Birkenlunden

YLAJALI (108 A4) (*ɯ H3*)
Exciting food at affordable prices. A new one-price set-meal is produced every week, inspired by the Mediterranean and France. *Mon–Sat from 5.30pm | St. Olavs plass 2 | tel. 22 20 64 86 | tram 17: Tullinløkka*

RESTAURANTS: BUDGET

INSIDER TIP ASYLET ● (115 D1) (*ɯ L4*)
The building from around 1730 was once a children's home, among other things, hence its name. Simple dishes such as *smørebrød* (sandwiches) and grilled salmon are served with beer in this dark historical restaurant and in the pretty court-

LOCAL SPECIALITIES

▶ **elgsteak** – elk steak served with vegetables and potato gratin

▶ **finnbiff** – thinly sliced reindeer meat with a sour-cream sauce and brown goats cheese

▶ **kjøttkaker** – meat balls in brown sauce (photo above left)

▶ **kokt torsk** – poached cod with potatoes and carrots

▶ **linje akevitt** – potato Aquavit is transported back and forth across the Equator and matures on the way in oak barrels. The label on the back tells you on which ship this potent Norwegian speciality sailed the seas

▶ **moltekrem** – cloudberries mixed with whipped cream

▶ **øl** – Norwegian beer is brewed in accordance with beer purity regulations. Lighter variants for the summer are called *sommerøl* or *skjærgårdsøl*

▶ **reker** – prawns served in summer with white bread, mayonnaise, lemon and white wine (photo above right)

▶ **rømmegrøt** – made with sour cream and milk. Tastes best with *spekemat*

▶ **saft** – juice made from blackcurrents (*solbær*) or other fruit. *Toddi* means it is served warm

▶ **spekemat** – cured pork, lamb (*fenalår*) and cold meat

▶ **tilslørte bondepiker** – 'farmer's daughter in a veil': a dessert made with roasted breadcrumbs, apple purée and whipped cream

▶ **vafler** – Norwegian waffles served with sour cream, brown goats cheese (*geitost*) or jam

▶ **vørterøl** – non-alcoholic, non-brewed drink made with water, malt and hops

yard at the back. *Grønland 28 | tel. 22 17 09 39 | T-bane 1–6: Grønland*

CURRY & KETCHUP RESTAURANT (106 C1) *(ᗕ F1)*
Uninspiring name, interesting food. The Indian menu is varied and cheap. The service and atmosphere are sometimes a bit hectic, but that is probably because there are always people waiting for a table. Tip: order a salad with your main meal – it's always fresh. *Kirkeveien 51 | tel. 22 69 05 22 | tram 12: Frogner Stadion*

JARLEN RESTAURANT
(109 F6) (*M5*)

Multicultural, as could be expected in Grønland. Traditional Norwegian and Danish dishes can be found on the menu as can pizza and chicken curry. Whale steak available on Sundays. Filling food and good service. *Åkebergveien 34 | tel. 22 67 76 80 | T-bane 1–6: Tøyen (10 mins. on foot)*

KITTY'S SUSHI (109 D2) (*K2*)

On a side road in the heart of trendy Grünerløkka serving delicious sushi, maki and sashimi. If you don't want to spend too much on a filling lunch, go for a wok dish or one of the sushi offers of the day. *Helgesens gate 14 | tel. 22 38 36 93 | www.kittys.no | tram 11, 12, 13: Olav Ryes plass*

LORRY ★ (107 E3) (*G2*)

Classic pub with more than 100 different types of beer, plain Norwegian food à la carte and a set lunch. Lively atmosphere and a meeting place for artists. *Parkveien 12 | tel. 22 69 69 04 | tram 11, 17, 18: Welhavens gate*

INSIDER TIP OLYMPEN MAT OG VINHUS ● (109 E6) (*L4*)

Anyone who knows Grønland will know this traditional restaurant as 'Lompa'. Generous helpings of reindeer, boiled cod and *sursild* (sour herring) are served here. *Grønlandsleiret 15 | tel. 24 10 19 99 | T-bane 1–6: Grønland*

INSIDER TIP SATGENE LUNSJBAR
(104 C5) (*0*)

This restaurant in the northeast of Oslo was thankfully saved from demolition and offers a warm welcome to young and old, neighbours and visitors from afar. Plain, good fare at affordable prices. *Maridalsveien 153 | tel. 98 44 89 00 | bus 20, 37, 54: Arendalsgata*

SCHRØDER RESTAURANT
(108 A3) (*H2*)

Informal, pub-like atmosphere with red-and-white tablecloths. This is where Harry Hole, the famous policeman in the crime novels written by Jo Nesbø, always hangs out. *Flesk og duppe* is just one of the typically Norwegian dishes on the menu. *Waldemar Thranes gate 8 | tel. 22 60 51 83 | bus 21, 37, 46: St. Hans-haugen*

VEGA ☺
(108 B4) (*J3*)

The most popular vegetarian restaurant in Oslo – cheap and centrally located – with food always prepared using fresh, organic, fair trade produce. Help yourself to dishes from around the world at the buffet. All-you-can-eat for just £10 (15US$); from noon–2.30pm during the week it is even cheaper. *Sun–Thu noon–8pm, Fri 11am–4pm | Akersgata 74 | tel. 22 67 76 80 | www.vegafairfood.no | bus 33, 37, 46: Rosingsgate*

LOW BUDGET

▶ You can even enjoy exotic food cheaply in expensive Oslo. There are many Asian restaurants and stands on Torggata that serve good food at an acceptable price – including vegetarian dishes. The best kebab on Oslo's 'kebab road' can be found at *Marino Grill* (108 A6) (*J4*) (*Torggata 29*).

▶ You don't have to be a student to eat for 50 NOK in the student canteen *Frederikke Mathus* (0) (*0*) in Blindern. *Mon–Thu 10am–7pm, Fri 10am–6pm | Problemveien 11 | T-bane 3, 4, 5: Blindern*

SHOPPING

🏙 **WHERE TO START**
📍 **(108 A–B 5–6) (📖 H–J4) Karl Johans gate:** In the side streets to the north and south of the boulevard in the city centre there are several shopping centres such as *Glasmagasinet* and *Steen & Strøm Magasin*. The luxury boutiques in Bogstadveien in *Frogner* are more exclusive and generally more expensive than in other countries, but still worth seeking out. In *Grønland* things are more exotic, colourful and cheaper, especially around *Grønlands torget*.

Lusekofte, the traditional cardigan with a black-and-white design (*luse* means 'lice') or a Norwegian pullover have long been popular souvenirs from the cool north. Another suitable present for men is the lesser known *busserull*. This striped farmer's shirt became a more acceptable item of clothing after academics with a penchant for life in the country started to wear them. Some people in Norway wear them on festive occasions now too. Cheese graters, Sami jewellery and crafts, reindeer pelts, silver or pewter Viking beakers and wooden mugs are firm favourites too. Oslo's large shopping centres in the centre are the perfect place in bad weather as well.

Photo: The selection of glass items in Oslo is huge

Glass, fish and *lusekofte* – traditional crafts and modern designer objects are popular in Oslo. But they come at a price

DESIGN & ART

DOGA NORSK DESIGN-OG ARKITEKTURSENTER ★
(108 C4) (*Ø K3*)
Exhibitions and a shop in a restored former transformer station right on the River Akerselva. DogA has prize-winning Norwegian designer objects and other items, books on architecture and much more.

Hausmannsgate 16 | www.doga.no | bus 34, 54: Jakob kirke

INSIDER TIP **KUNSTNERFORBUNDET** ●
(113 E1) (*Ø H4*)
150 contemporary Norwegian artists run a gallery behind the Rådhuset where works on display can also be bought. *Kjeld Stubs gate 3 | www.kunstnerforbundet.no | tram 12: Rådhusplassen*

'Fiske Nilsen' is Oslo's oldest fish shop and enough to make any fish fan's heart beat faster

NORWAY DESIGNS (107 F5) (*H4*)

Textiles, glasswork and jewellery with modern Norwegian designs are available at Norway Designs. The artistic glass in particular is exquisite. *Stortingsgata 28 | www.norwaydesigns.no | T-bane 1–6, tram 13, 19: Nationaltheatret*

ROM FOR IDÉ (104 A6) (*O*)

Think-tank for Norwegian furniture designers in a former dairy in the Majorstuen district. The gallery also displays crafted items and the staff are happy to take time to advise customers. Shipping service also available. *Jacob Aals gate 54 | www.rom foride.no | tram 11,12,19: Majorstuent*

SHOPPING STREETS & CENTRES

BOGSTADVEIEN ★
(107 D2) (*F–G 1–2*)

The shops between the royal park and Majorstua are devilishly expensive. From exclusive greengrocers, exquisite fashion boutiques and shoe shops to the Helly Hansen brand store, almost everything can be found on Bogstadveien. *Frogner | www. bogstadveien.no | tram 11, 19: Rosenborg*

GRØNLAND ★ (109 D6) (*K–L4*)

Immigrants from around the world, especially from Pakistan, characterise this colourful district and what is sold here. Bollywood films, clothes from *Sheikhs Fashion,* vegetables from *Batat Import* – everything can be found on or near the square *Grønlands torget*. Visit the new bazaar and glimpse the mosque's minarets from a distance and you too will feel miles away from a Scandinavian capital! *www. gronlandstorg.no | T-bane 1–6: Grønland*

STEEN & STRØM MAGASIN ●
(114 A2) (*J4*)

The most famous shopping centre in Oslo has been providing the Norwegian capital with goods from the rest of Europe since

1797. It has recently been renovated and is home to shops selling women's clothes, sports articles, perfume and food. The selection is exclusive with prices that match. *Kongensgate 23 | www.steenogstrom.no | bus 30, 60, 70: Kongensgate*

VIKA TERRASSEN
(113 D1) (*ØØ G4*)

Oslo's most beautiful and most centrally located row of shops. The Vika Terrassen below the Foreign Office is home to 15 fashion stores – all top international labels for clothes and shoes. The tram stop on line 12 and the National Theatre are just 2 mins. on foot. And what is even nicer: the staff in these boutiques take a lot of time for their customers. The many restaurants and a spa centre round off the shopping experience here. *Ruseløkkveien 26*

FISH

Smoked fish can easily be transported. Smoked salmon is a good bet and quality fish can also be found in supermarkets. But always check the sell-by-date on vacuum-packed food. If you come across salmon smoked with *einebær* (juniper), don't hesitate to snap it up. Other less well-known specialities include *røkt kolje* (smoked shellfish) and *røkt blåkveite* (smoked Greenland halibut). Fshmongers will also vacuum-pack fish for you (normally free of charge).

LAKSEN FISK OG VILT
(105 D5) (*ØØ 0*)

Unfortunately a little distance from the centre, but one of Oslo's best fishmongers. Also sells homemade produce other than fish and venison such as herring salad, lingonberry jam and cloudberry cream. *Maridalsveien 188 | www.laksen. no | bus 37, 54: Advokat Dehlis plass*

INSIDER TIP **GEORG NILSEN FISK & VILT** (107 D2) (*ØØ F1*)

'Fiske Nilsen' is Oslo's oldest fish shop with the best selection of fish and game. Just the sight of what is on offer is an eye-opener. How about picking up a small bag of *klippfisk* – dried and salted fish which is used to make a delicious fish stew called *bacalhau* with potatoes, onions, olive oil, tomatos and peppers? Recipes available in the shop. *Bogstadveien 39 | www.georg anilsen.no | tram 11, 19: Schultz gate*

MARCO POLO HIGHLIGHTS

★ **DogA Norsk Design- og Arkitektursenter**
More aesthetic than practical but a delight to the eye
→ p. 59

★ **Bogstadveien**
Shopping street where money does not play a role
→ p. 60

★ **Grønland**
Exotic rather than exclusive in Oslo's multicultural corner
→ p. 60

★ **Husfliden**
From cheese graters to local costumes – this is where you'll find traditional Norwegian products from all corners of the country
→ p. 62

★ **Juhls' Silvergallery**
Norway's most famous silver jewellery inspired by the light and expanse of the northern Norwegian *vidda* is – fortunately – also available in Oslo → p. 63

GLASS & CERAMICS

GLASS & CERAMICS

INSIDER TIP **BRUDD** (108 C3) *(ΜΩ K2)*
A form of cooperative comprising 20 artists selling imaginatively made ceramics, glass and other crafts. *Markveien 42 A | www.brudd.info | tram 11, 12, 13: Schous plass*

GLASMAGASINET
(108 B6) *(ΜΩ J4)*
A feast for the senses can be had on the ground floor in the shopping centre on the market square behind the cathedral: glass, cut glass and porcelain as well as a confectionary and wonderful smells. The famous Norwegian glassblower Hadeland has a branch here too. *Stortorvet 9 | www.glasmagasinet.no | tram 11, 17, 18: Stortorvet*

GLAZED & AMUSED ●
(108 C2) *(ΜΩ K2)*
Pottery lovers will have lots of fun in this gallery and workshop – as you can have a go yourself here too and experiment with different colours and glazes. Allow around 2 hours. Your piece however won't be properly dry until 1 week later. *Markveien 25 | www.glazedandamused. no | tram 11, 12, 13: Olav Ryes plass*

NORWEGIAN PRODUCTS

HEIMEN (108 A5) *(ΜΩ H4)*
Norwegian *husflid* – various handmade products – are on sale right next to *Hotell Bondeheimen*: traditional costumes and *lusekofte, busserull* shirts and both traditional and modern Norwegian jewellery. *Rosenkrantz gate 8 | www.heimen.net | tram 11, 17, 18: Tinghuset*

HUSFLIDEN ★
(108 B6) *(ΜΩ J4)*
Here, you will find traditional costumes from all the different regions in Norway to admire or buy. Other handmade items are also available such as jewellery, pretty and practical things made of wood, elk slippers and reindeer pelts. *Stortorvet 9 | on the lower level in Glasmagasinet | www. dennorskehusfliden.no | tram 11, 17, 18: Stortorvet*

SPORTSNETT
(113 E1) *(ΜΩ H4)*
The great outdoors is part of the Norwegian identity. Whether you want to trek to the North Pole or simply go on a long hike – you will find everything you need

LOW BUDGET

▶ The second-hand chain *Fretex* (108 C2) *(ΜΩ K1)* run by the Salvation Army sells everything from sports articles to evening dresses and, with a bit of luck, you may be able to pick up a Norwegian pullover or other typically Norwegian things (*Markveien 5 | www.fretex.no | tram 11, 12, 13: Birkelunden*). Norwegian glass for everyday use and pictures can be found in the second-hand shop *Maritas Bruktbutikk* (108 C4) *(ΜΩ K3)*. Profits go to help fight drug adiction. *Markveien 67 | www.marita. no | tram 11, 12, 13: Nybrua*

▶ Up to 30 market tenders set up their stalls every day on Oslo's 'Red Square' (114 B1) *(ΜΩ J4)* – where the Social Democrats and Unions have their offices. You can find anything here from Norwegian CDs to locally produced honey and military memorabilia – often at low prices. *Youngstorget | tram 11, 12, 13, 17: Brugata*

Perhaps not the most original of presents, but certainly the warmest: the Norwegian pullover

here. *Olav V's gate 6 | www.sportsnett.no | bus 30, 70, tram 13, 19, T-bane 1–6: Nationaltheatret*

VINMONOPOLET (108 C3) *(𝄞 K2–3)*

Wine and spirits are only available in state-run Vinmonopolet stores, most of which are self-service. The traditional atmosphere with long queues of patient customers who are served by sales staff in uniform can still be found in the *Vinmonopolet* in Grünerløkka, where you can also buy your bottle of *Linje Akevitt –* true to style but expensive. By the way, this branch is on the premises once occupied by *Beckers,* formerly one of the most famous pubs in the city. *Nordre gate 16, Ecke Markveien | www.vinmonopolet. no | tram 11, 12, 13: Olaf Ryes plass*

YOUNGSTORGET, STORTORVET, KARL JOHANS GATE (114 B1–2) *(𝄞 J4)*

There are many souvenir shops and, in summer, market stands on the squares

in the city centre that sell Norwegian souvenirs. But be careful: the 'Norwegian' pullovers are often made in China!

SILVER & JEWELLERY

JUHLS' SILVERGALLERY ★
(113 E1) *(𝄞 H4)*

Sami jewellery and crafts from the north of Norway and the tundra region can be found at Juhls' Silvergallery where they also stock glassware from the far north. *Roald Amundsens gate 6 | www.juhls.no | tram 13, 19, T-bane 1–6: Nationaltheatret*

THUNE (113 F1) *(𝄞 H4)*

There are many branches of Norway's best-known and largest jeweller's in the capital. The one on the corner of Egertorget Square and Karl Johans gate was established in 1861. They stock a huge range of classical jewellery and watches. *Øvre Slottsgate 12 | www.thune.no | tram 12, 13, 19: Wessels plass*

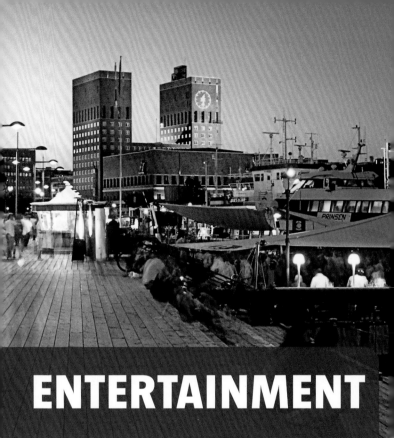

ENTERTAINMENT

WHERE TO START

CITY **WHERE TO START**
Youngstorget (114 B1) *(〽 J4)*, north of the cathedral and the eastern end of Karl Johans gate, is the heart and soul of the labour movement in Norway. Pubs and bars – more cosy or tatty than elegant – crowd around the square. There are also some good clubs in the vicinity. And those who fancy a drink overlooking the water will find what they are looking for on popular **Aker Brygge (113 D2)** *(〽 G5)* right on Oslo Fjord.

Everyone knows that alcohol is expensive in Norway. For this reason many people in Oslo have a drink at home before going out to their favourite café – that is often a pub – or bar.

And there are enough of these in Oslo. The same is true of clubs and concert venues. Oslo is quick to pick up on trends and to create new ones. The city has a lot to offer from a musical point of view. Free concerts and a continuous string of new pubs turn any balmy summer evening into an event. By law it is forbidden to serve spirits to those under 20 years of age in Norway which is why lots of clubs, bars and discos have a minimum age of 20. And there is a fixed

Photo: Popular Aker Brygge on a midsummer's night

Live is always best: the night in Oslo's music venues, cool clubs and cosy cafés kicks off to jazz, rock and classical music

closing time too. At 3.30am at the latest all pubs and restaurants have to close.

BALLET/CONCERTS/THEATRE

INSIDER TIP DANSENS HUS
(108 C3) (*𝕄 K2*)

Modern dance has its home in a former factory in Grünerløkka. Performances given by national and international dance com-

panies are of a continuously high standard. *Tickets: tel. 23 70 94 00 or Mon–Fri 4pm–8pm, Sat/Sun from 2 hrs. before the beginning of a performance | Møllerveien 2 | www.dansenshus.com | bus 34, 54, tram 11, 12, 13: Møllerveien*

KONSERTHUSET (113 D–E1) (*𝕄 G4*)
The Oslo Philharmonic Orchestra is based in this bastion of classical music where

A feast for the eyes and a delight for the ears: the acoustics in Oslo's opera house are also superb

world-famous and national performers such as the pianist Leif Ove Andsnes and the trumpeter Ole Edvard Antonsen regularly appear as guests. *Tickets: tel. 23 11 31 11 | Mon–Fri 11am–5pm, Sat 11am–2pm | Munkedamsveien 14 | www.oslokonsert hus.no | tram 12: Aker Brygge, 13, 19: Nationaltheatret*

DEN NORSKE OPERA OG NASJONALBALLETT ★
(114 C3) (*𝄞 J–K5*)

Right in the middle of Oslo's complex of streets – there it is, an expanse of gleaming white marble stretching all the way down into the fjord. The monumental opera house with its two stages is home to the state opera and the national ballet companies. According to experts, the acoustics are among the best in the world. The price of tickets varies from 140–1600 kroner. *Ticket office in the entrance hall Mon–Fri 9am–8pm, Sat 11am–6pm, Sun noon–6pm | Kirsten Flagstads plass 1 | tel. 8154 44 88 | www.operaen.no | all T-bane lines: Oslo S*

BARS

INSIDER TIP ▸ BAR BOCA
(109 D2) (*𝄞 K2*)

There's a whole lettuce in the Bloody Mary and the *mojito* is considered the best in town. The retro styled Bar Boca is very small but has a few seats for smokers outside on the pavement too. *Thorvald Meyers gate 30 | tram 11, 12, 13: Olaf Ryes plass*

BIBLIOTEKSBAREN (113 F1) (*𝄞 H4*)

Classic, dark hotel bar with chandeliers and deep chesterfields. This is where the elite from the worlds of finance and culture meet for a chat over a pint of beer. An eternally young pianist plays away in the background. *Kristian IV's gate 7 | tram 12, 13, 19: Stortorvet*

HANNIBALS HYBEL ★
(113 D2) (*𝄞 G5*)

A genuine pub on Aker Brygge where beer is served in half-litre glasses (while others use .4 litre ones). And, as you can sit on

building between the station and Grønland is where the cultural bohème meet. You can only have a drink here and a few peanuts but you will always find a quiet corner for a relaxing conversation. *Tøyenbekken 34 | www.oslomekaniskeverksted. no | tram 18, 19: Bussterminalen Grønland*

CLUBS & DISCOS

CAFE MONO (108 B5) (*J4*)
The customers here are not worried if you are fashionably dressed or not. The café's style and music – from jazz to country, rock to Indi-pop, underline it's genuine feel. *Min. age 22 | Pløensgate 4 | www.cafe mono.no*

the quayside here, this is the best place on really warm and late summer evenings. *Aker Brygge | tram 12: Aker Brygge*

JUSTISEN (114 B1) (*J4*)
In the rambling rooms where coffins were once made, lawyers, civil servants and politicians now meet. Garden restaurant in a lovely courtyard. *Møllergaten 15 | tel. 22 42 24 72 | www.justisen.no | tram 12, 13, 19: Stortorvet*

LITTERATURHUSET ★ ●
(107 E4) (*G3*)
Oslo's literature house has been in this former teaching college on the edge of the royal park since 2007. The café which offers healthy dishes, delicious drinks and a friendly crowd can be highly recommended. *Wergelandsveien 2 | www.litteratur huset.no | tram 11: Welhavens gate*

OSLO MEKANISKE VERKSTED
(115 D2) (*K4*)
Nobody has tried to cover up this building's past as a metalworker's studio. This brick

MARCO POLO HIGHLIGHTS

★ **Den Norske Opera og Nasjonalballett**
Oslo's building of the century provides the very best of culture for everyone → p. 66

★ **Hannibals Hybel**
Despite its up-market location on Aker Brygge it almost has the atmosphere of a harbour pub when guests have a pint before catching their ferry home → p. 66

★ **Litteraturhuset**
The literature house is a lovely place to enjoy a relaxed conversation or an intellectual discussion over a drink and a salad → p. 67

★ **Blå**
It's worth the wait: live acts for the initiated in this internationally renowned music venue → p. 69

CINEMAS

INSIDER TIP ▶ DATTERA TIL HAGEN
(115 D1) (𝒨 K4)

'Hagen's Daughter' extends over two floors. Downstairs, you can tuck into burgers, pasta dishes, sandwiches and tapas; upstairs concerts and other performances are held. An intimate and lively club in Grønland. *Grønland 10 | tel. 22 17 18 70 | www.dattera.no | T-bane 1–6: Grønland*

INSIDER TIP ▶ HERR NILSEN ●
(114 A1) (𝒨 H4)

Jazz for everyone is the club's motto. The décor is traditional. When there are no concerts, Herr Nilsen is a normal bar and café. *C. J. Hambros plass | www.herrnilsen. no | tram 11, 17, 18: Tinghuset*

INTERNASJONALEN (114 B1) (𝒨 J4)

On Oslo's 'Red Square' where the Social Democrats and trade unions have their offices, a music club can only really have one name: 'The International'. Harmony is not the name of the game but rock music instead. Beer is served outside until 3am. *Youngstorget 2 | www.internasjonalen.no | tram 11, 12, 13, 17: Brugata*

SMUGET (113 E–F1) (𝒨 H4)

A bar, disco, concert and stand-up comedy venue – Smuget is four things in one. Some 700 cultural events are held on the two stages here every year. An Oslo institution. *Rosenkrantz' gate 22 | www. smuget.no | tram 12: Rådhusplassen*

SOUND OF MU (108 C4) (𝒨 K3)

The not-so-young gather here in this little bar with its minimalistic décor. A club that doesn't fit in any pigeonhole with concerts and exhibitions, matinées and readings. *Markveien 58 | www.soundofmu. no | tram 11, 12, 13: Nybrua*

CAFÉ SØR (114 B1) (𝒨 J4)

A café with delicious sandwiches by day, then a cocktail bar and ultimately a dance venue. Depending on the day of the week, the DJs play all sorts of different music. Things are pretty relaxed here yet at some time everyone breaks out in a sweat. *Torggata 11 | www.cafesor.no | tram 11, 12, 13, 17: Brugata*

LOW BUDGET

▶ *Evergreen Inn* **(107 F4)** *(𝒨 H3)* has Oslo's cheapest beer – just 30 kroner before 9pm. Even later it's still affordable too. *Pilestredet 39 | in the university complex*

▶ There are many ● *free pop, rock and folk concerts* on the square outside the city hall, **(113 E2)** *(𝒨 H4–5)*, for example. Details from the Tourist Information Office or in the free magazine 'What's on in Oslo' published every two months. *www.visitoslo.com/en/your-oslo/ on-a-budget/events* also tells you what's on

▶ Matinées and concerts are held regularly in and around the opera house **(114 C3)** *(𝒨 J–K5)*. Free entrance. There's something on every day – that's what the director of the opera house promised! So keep your eyes peeled.

CINEMAS

Most films are shown in the original language with Norwegian subtitles. What is being screened where can be seen under *www.oslokino.no,* where you can also buy tickets *(100 NOK | tel. 82 05 00 01).*

One evening it's dance music, the next avant-garde – Blå is always good for a surprise

CINEMATEKET (114 B2) (*m J5*)

Amateur, old, alternative and Norwegian films are shown in the Cinemateket, the Norwegian Film Institute's film club with an adjoining film museum (free entrance with an English guidebook) and a shop for Norwegian films. *Dronningens gate 16 | www.nfi.no/cinemateket | tram 12, 13, 19: Dronningens gate*

LIVE MUSIC

INSIDER TIP BETONG (106 C1) (*m F1*)

Concert hall in the 1970s'-style Student Union building with a large concrete tower. The theatre inside is cosy. *Betong* has since become one of the most important concert venues in Oslo. *Slemdalsveien 15 | www.studentersamfundet.no/lokaler.php? lokale=Betong | T-bane 1–6: Majorstuen*

BLÅ ★ (108 C4) (*m K3*)

One evening it's dance music, the next avant-garde – just check it out! Jazz and other music is performed in this club that the BBC named one of the best music venues in Europe. As a result, long queues are common. *Brenneriveien 9 c | www. blaaoslo.no | bus 34, 54: Møllerveien*

GLORIA FLAMES (113 D1) (*m K4*)

One of those clubs that tirelessly provides a platform for Oslo's music scene. Rock or Indi-pop are popular but the boundaries between music genres are there to be crossed. Concerts are held on the terrace in summer. *Grønland 18 | www.gloria flames.no | T-bane 1–6: Grønland*

PARKTEATRET (109 D3) (*m K2*)

Jazz, rock, blues and a documentary film cinema – Parkteatret is all of these things. Originally built as a cinema, Grünerløkka's local scene now meets in front of the building. *Olaf Ryes plass 11 | www.parkteatret. no | tram 11, 12, 13: Olaf Ryes plass*

ROCKEFELLER (108 B5) (*m J4*)

Two large stages and a pub are a guarantee for lots of music in Rockefeller. The stages and the *John Dee Live Club & Pub* are in the former Torggata indoor swimming pool building. *Torggata 16 | www.rockefeller.no | tram 11, 12, 13, 17, bus 30, 34, 54: Brugata*

WHERE TO STAY

Staying the night in one of the most expensive cities in the world is obviously not going to be cheap, you might well think. But that's not quite true. Despite generally high prices, there are also guesthouses and hostels in the Norwegian capital for tighter budgets too.

Like many major cities, Oslo also has a lot of medium category hotels – mostly international hotel chains with their familiar furnishings and little individual appeal. These are mainly aimed at business people but attract tourists from around the world in the summer with special rates and packages. If you book early, you may well be able to find a room in one of Oslo's luxury hotels for just £135/210US$ that will certainly cost more at other times. And luxury is not just a question of the furnishings, atmosphere or restaurants: a hotel should also be quietly situated and have perfect service as well as being close to the city centre. But if you are prepared to make a few concessions, you can also find a room in pricey Oslo that is relatively cheap.

Most simple accommodation is a little way from the centre and Karl Johans gate. But it is very easy to find your way around the Norwegian capital and it has an extensive public transport network. If you buy a ticket valid for several journeys you can

Photo: The Kari Traa room in the Grand Hotel

From a cosmopolitan designer hotel to a wooden castle in the country – Oslo's hotels offer as much variety as the city itself

save on hotel costs. And many of the more modest hotels often have extensive breakfast buffets too that will keep you going for most of the day while sightseeing in the Norwegian capital. Virtually all hotels in Oslo, regardless of category, now have Wi-Fi access in the rooms.

Although new hotels are continuously being built, in the peak season in July and August demand exceeds capacity. Advance booking is absolutely essential *(www.visit oslo.com/en* then use link *'book online here: Hotel'* on right).

HOTELS: EXPENSIVE

CLARION COLLECTION HOTELL FOLKETEATRET (114 C1) (*ﬞﾉ K4*)

Oslo's new top address. Modern and stylish hotel near the main station with a break-

fast buffet that has already made a name for itself. The foyer and rooms are especially attractive; the noise of the city is completely shut out. The gym area, styled on a 1930s New York boxing studio, is a unique feature. *160 rooms | Storgaten 21–23 | tel. 22 00 57 00 | www.clarionhotel. com/hotel-oslo-norway-NO111 | tram 11, 12, 13, 17: Brugata*

Grims Grenka: designed from top to toe – including the name

INSIDER TIP **GRIMS GRENKA**
(114 A2) *(Ⓜ H5)*
Even the name of this hotel that opened in 2008 is part of the design and doesn't mean anything. While you may well expect light and bright colours in a Scandinavian hotel, the clear but austere lines of the Grims Grenka are generally in darker shades. Various summertime moods can be created in the 'Summer Room' using a special light installation. *50 rooms | Kongensgate 5 | tel. 23 10 72 00 | www. grimsgrenka.no | bus 60: Bankplassen, tram 12, 13, 19: Kongens gate*

HOLMENKOLLEN PARK HOTEL RICA ★ ● ⚕ (116 B6) *(Ⓜ 0)*
Just a stone's throw from the Holmenkollen ski arena is this hotel that looks like a fairy-tale castle made of wood. The oldest part dates from the 19th century when the inn was built in the National Romantic 'dragon style' inspired by stave churches. Rural romanticism in its purest form paired with first-class service and a very good restaurant. And to top it all: a panoramic view over Oslo and the fjord. *222 rooms | Kongeveien 26 | tel. 22 92 20 00 | www.holmenkollenparkhotel.no | T-bane 1: Holmenkollen*

OPERA HOTEL
(114 C2) *(Ⓜ K5)*
Perfect for those travelling by train or coach! The hotel is just behind the station and Jernbanetorget junction with the opera house on the other side of the road on the quayside. Understated atmosphere rather marked by its popularity as a business hotel. *434 rooms | Christian Frederiks plass 5 | tel. 24 10 30 00 | www.thonhotels. no/opera | bus 32, 34, 74, 83: Jernbanetorget*

SCANDINAVIA HOTEL
(107 F4) *(Ⓜ H3)*
The name has changed, but for most locals it is and remains the Hotel on the Royal Park, the SAS Hotel (Scandinavian Airlines). With 22 storeys it's not as high as the Plaza but high enough to tower

over the palace and the Norwegian royals. A drink in the ☼ bar on the 21st floor is the perfect way to round off a sightseeing tour of Oslo. *488 rooms | Holbergs gate 30 | tel. 23 29 30 00 | www.radissonblu. com/scandinaviahotel-oslo | airport bus from hotel, tram 11, 17, 18: Holbergs plass*

HOTELS: MODERATE

HOTEL ASTORIA
(114 B2) (*ⓜ J4*)
Who needs more: the location is perfect (50m from Karl Johans gate, 300m from the station), the furnishing in the rooms is functional. There are family rooms and rooms for allergy sufferers. Cheaper still if you book online well in advance. *180 rooms | Dronningens gate 21 | tel. 24 14 55 50 | www.thonhotels.no/astoria | all bus, tram and T-bane lines, near Oslo S*

HOTEL BONDEHEIMEN
(108 A5) (*ⓜ H4*)
The theatres, nightlife and cultural hotspots are just around the corner. In the olden days, people from the country used to stay at Bondeheimen whenever they came to town. Even after comprehensive renovation, the Bondeheimen still retains much of its countrified Norwegian style. As a city hotel it is reasonably priced; at weekends however there are often lots of seminar and congress guests. *127 rooms | Rosenkrantz' gate 8 | tel. 23 21 41 00 | www.bondeheimen.com | tram 11, 17, 18: Tinghuset*

HOTEL GABELSHUS ★
(106 B6) (*ⓜ E4*)
If you're looking for a quiet, elegant hotel then the Gabelshus is the place for you. Located slightly off the beaten track in up-market Frogner to the west of the city centre. The façade is clad in ivy like a classic English building. Inside it has an elegant

charm of its own. Near the Baltic ferry terminal. *114 rooms | Gabels gate 16 | tel. 23 27 65 00 | www.gabelshus.no | tram 13: Skillebekk*

HOTEL GYLDENLØVE
(107 D2) (*ⓜ G2*)
The Hotel Gyldenløve has been transformed into a modern Norwegian designer hotel. Originally built in the Functionalist style, it is located in Oslo's most exclusive and popular shopping street half way between the Royal Park and Vigeland Park. *164 rooms | Bogstadveien 20 | tel. 23 33 23 00 | www.thonhotels.no/ gyldenlove | tram 11, 19: Rosenborg*

QUALITY HOTEL 33 ★
(0) (*ⓜ 0*)
This 1960s-style designer hotel is a little distance from the centre. Simple, clear lines characterise the design of the rooms.

★ **Holmenkollen Park Hotel Rica**
Undiluted Norwegian wooden architecture and a wonderful view of the fjord → **p. 72**

★ **Hotel Gabelshus**
Especially stylish accommodation for a medium category hotel → **p. 73**

★ **Quality Hotel 33**
Lots of space right up to the glass top floor. This is where you can really find peace and quiet! → **p. 73**

★ **Grand Hotel**
Elegance and art in every nook and cranny → **p. 74**

MARCO POLO HIGHLIGHTS

A restaurant, bar and relaxation area are on the ☘ top floor which offers a fantastic view of Oslo Fjord. *242 rooms | Østre Aker vei 33 | tel. 23 19 33 33 | www.choice hotels.no | bus 60: Økern næringspark*

RICA HOTEL G20
(114 A1) (*ω J4*)
Although this is a typical business hotel, it is a good alternative in summer for those exploring the city. Modern, functional design, perfectly situated just 500m from the station. Friendly and efficient service. The rooms are a bit on the small side, but the breakfast is excellent. *96 rooms | Grensen 20 | tel. 22 31 06 11 | www.rica.no/hoteller/g20 | tram 11, 17, 18: Tinghuset*

HOTEL SAVOY
(108 A5) (*ω H3*)
This hotel, steeped in tradition, is right next to the National Gallery. The 4-storey hotel has 93 cosy rooms. The *Bar des Savoy* is a popular meeting place at weekends which means it can also get a bit loud at times. *Universitetsgata 11 | tel. 23 35*

LUXURY HOTELS

Bristol (108 A5) (*ω H4*)
Built in the 1920s with a new wing added in 2000. The hotel's traditionally dark décor can best be seen in the *Bristol Grill* where chandeliers hang from the ceiling and sabres decorate the walls. The ● *Bibliothek Bar* is a popular meeting place for artists and authors. When booking, ask for a room on one of the upper floors as the traffic can be unpleasantly loud especially at weekends. *251 rooms | £140–315/170–500US$ | Kristian IV's gate 7 | tel. 22 82 60 00 | www.thonhotels.no/bristol | tram 11, 17, 18: Tinghuset*

Continental ☘ (107 F5) (*ω H4*)
Norway's best-known hotel is in Stortingsgata right opposite the National Theatre. The equally well-known *Theatercafé* is located on the ground floor of this traditional hotel. The Continental has been in the ownership of the same family now for four generations and the leading ladies have all left their very distinctive stamps on the hotel. None of the rooms are the same, all are furnished with antiques and emphasis placed on individuality. The hotel is the only one in Norway to belong to the 'Leading Hotels of the World'. *155 rooms | £140–315/170–500US$ | Stortingsgata 24–26 | tel. 22 82 40 00 | www.hotel-continental.com | tram 13, 19, T-bane 1–6: Nationaltheatret*

Grand Hotel ★ (108 A6) (*ω H4*)
Every year in December a new Nobel Prize winner waves to the people of Oslo from the balcony of his elegant suite; during the rest of the year international stars from the film and music industry stay here. The famous hotel opposite the parliament building on Karl Johans gate has 54 suites and 238 rooms. One curiosity is the 'Ladies Floor' with 13 rooms reserved for ladies only, furnished in a suitably feminine style and with its own spa. *£150–315/233–500US$ | Karl Johans gate 31 | tel. 23 21 20 00 | www.grand.no | T-bane 1–6: Stortinget, tram 13, 19: Wesselsplass*

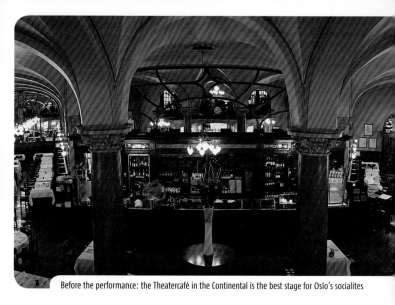

Before the performance: the Theatercafé in the Continental is the best stage for Oslo's socialites

42 00 | www.choicehotels.no | tram 11, 17, 18: Tullinløkka

INSIDER TIP **VILLA FROGNER BED & BREAKFAST** (106 C3) (*ø E2*)
One of Oslo's nicest medium category hotels can be found in a quiet side street right on Frogner Park. The large rooms are beautifully furnished and the breakfast room is conducive to getting to know other guests. *Nordraaksgate 26 | tel. 22 56 19 60 | www.bedandbreakfast.no | tram no. 12: Vigelandsparken*

HOTELS: BUDGET

ANKER HOTEL
(107 D5) (*ø K3*)
For those who don't mind being a little distance from the city centre – and all the closer to the popular district of Grünerløkka, the Anker Hotel is a good choice. 161 bright and cheerful but simply furnished rooms in a massive building right on the River Akerselva. *Storgata 55 | tel. 22 99 75 00 | www.anker-hotel.no | bus 30, 31, tram 11, 12, 13, 17: Hausmanns gate*

COCHS PENSJONAT
(107 E4) (*ø G3*)
Modern but simply furnished rooms in a hotel near the palace. Not all 88 rooms are en-suite. Breakfast is not included in the price. However, overnight guests are given a discount for the breakfast buffet in the student café next door. *Parkveien 25 | tel. 23 33 24 00 | www.cochspensjonat.no | tram 12: Welhavens gate*

EMMA GJESTEHUS
(115 E3) (*ø 0*)
For those who come to Oslo by car, this place in the countryside near Oslo Fjord is a good choice. Guests who come from all over the world can use the kitchen to make their own meal in this simple but very cosy B&B. *Høyrabben 4 | 1366 Satndvika | tel. 67 13 06 59 | www.emmagjestehus.no |*

Famous name, modest prices: the Hotel Munch is a pleasant place to stay without any frills

on the E 16, approx. 25 mins. west of the city centre

HOTEL MUNCH (108 A5) *(ⓜ H3)*
Munch's paintings may be expensive but the hotel of the same name offers quality at an affordable price. 180 rooms of varying sizes, simply but stylishly furnished. Extensive breakfast buffet. The hotel is centrally located behind the government district. *Munchs gate 5 | tel. 23 21 96 00 | www.thonhotels.no/munch | tram 11, 17, 18: Tinghuset*

PERMINALEN (113 F2) *(ⓜ H4)*
A classic among Oslo's cheaper hotels. From the end of the 1960s this rather shabby building was used by soldiers on service or on their weekend breaks. Now it's a meeting place for backpackers from around the world. 1–6 bed rooms, better youth hostel standard. Perfect location between Stortinget and Akershus Fortress. *55 rooms | Øvre Slottsgate 2 | tel. 24 00 55 00 | www.perminalen.com | bus 30, 31, 32, 54: Kongensgate*

INSIDER TIP ▶ RESIDENCE KRISTINELUND (106 A4) *(ⓜ D3)*
Live like the wealthy residents in the west of the city but much more cheaply. The B&B in the Residence Kristinelund makes it possible. The villa, built in 1916, is on the edge of the diplomatic district at the end of Bygdøy Allee. The city centre is quite a distance but Bygdøy museum island and all its sights is that much closer. *24 rooms | Kristinelundsveien 2 | tel. 40 00 24 11 | www.kristinelund.no | bus 20, 30, 31: Olav Kyrres plass*

PRIVATE ACCOMMODATION & FLATS

B & B STORGATA

There's always room in even the smallest of spaces. In this case a pull-out sofa bed in a mini flat on the southern edge of Grünerløkka. But for that, there's a perfect all-round service – from being met at the station (10 mins. on foot) to lunch together (100 NOK extra). Only suitable for one person. *For more information see www.airbnb.com, then enter: Oslo, Storgata | Budget*

FROGNER HOUSE APARTMENTS

3 different buildings and some 100 different flats that all have one thing in common: style! You can make yourself at home here and, thanks to the central location, organise your holiday as you please. *Tel. 93 01 00 09 | Skovveien 8 (106 C5) (ฌ F3); Arbinsgate 3 (107 E5) (ฌ G4); Ullevålsveien 1 (108 B4) (ฌ J3) | Frognerhouse.no | Moderate*

YOUTH HOSTELS & SIMILAR

INSIDERTIP BUDGET HOTEL
(114 B2) (ฌ J5)

The top address in Oslo for backpackers: simple standard in small but clean and functional rooms at cheap rates in a pretty, elegant building plumb in the middle of things between the opera house and Karl Johans gate. If you book early, you only pay £24/37US$ a night. *54 rooms | Prinsens gate 6 | tel. 21 01 40 55 | www. budgethotel.no | all bus, tram and T-bane lines, near Oslo S*

VANDRERHJEM HARALDSHEIM
(105 F5) (ฌ O)

The rooms are rather like cabins on the ferry to Oslo but this youth hostel is located high up in Grefsen almost on the edge of the city. *69 beds from £27.50/ 43US$ a night/bed | Haraldsheimveien 4 | tel. 22 22 29 65 | www.haraldsheim.no | bus 31, 32, tram 17: Sinsenkrysset, T-bane 4, 6: Sinsen*

INSIDERTIP VANDRERHJEM HOLTEKILEN (O) (ฌ O)

Superb position on Oslo Fjord to the west of the city – well worth the 15-min. train ride. The price (from £24/37US$ per person) includes breakfast and lots of green in the surrounding area. *200 beds | Michelets vei 55 | tel. 67 51 80 40 | www. hihostels.no/no/Vandrerhjem/Ostlandet/ Oslo_Holtekilen | bus 151, 153, 161, 162, 252, 261 from the city centre: Kveldsroveien, Drammen train from Oslo S: Stabekk*

LOW BUDGET

▶ Small, simple cabins can be rented on *Bogstad Campingplatz* **(117 E2)** *(ฌ O)* to the west of Holmenkollen (from £43/68US$). The bus stops right outside the campsite. *Ankerveien 117 | tel. 22 51 08 00 | www.bogstad camping.no | bus 32: Bogstad Camping*

▶ Thanks to the Norwegian *Allemannsretten* – the right to roam – camping is also allowed on state-owned property if you observe certain simple rules. So buy a day ticket and head for the island *Hovedøya*, for example, choose a spot on a bay with a view of the city and spend the night in your tent – or in a sleeping bag under the stars. Oslo in the light of a summer's night and the early morning sun are an unforgettable picture postcard scene!

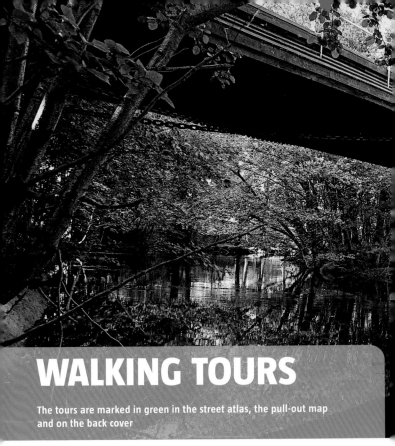

WALKING TOURS

The tours are marked in green in the street atlas, the pull-out map and on the back cover

1

TRACING OSLO'S INDUSTRIAL PAST ALONG IDYLLIC RIVERBANKS

Leave the touristy city centre behind you, explore the natural urban environment and, at the same time, find out about Norway's industrial past – this can all be done on a short 2½-hour walk which can easily be extended to half a day if you take a closer look at the sights en route. The little River Akerselva was the main industrial artery of industrial Christiania (Oslo) from the 16th century onwards. At first, sawmills and paper factories lined both banks, joined later by workshops and textile companies. Many of the former industrial buildings are now occupied by high-tech businesses and cultural enterprises and the river banks and surrounding areas along the whole stretch have developed into a paradise for nature-lovers and sports enthusiasts, as well as for culture vultures too. Don't forget your swimming things on a lovely summer's day!

The walks starts at Grønland underground station (T-bane 1–6) and follows the right bank of the river. Shortly after leaving the concrete station area behind you, a contrasting picture opens up that is so typical of the districts along the Akerselva. On one side of the river there are industrial

Photo: Åmot suspension bridge

Exploring Oslo and tracing its history –
whether industrial, maritime or sporting –
is always a great outdoor experience too

buildings and trade parks whereas, on the other side, there is a park-like landscape and open country.

Pass under Hausmann Bridge and on to **Anker Bridge** where it's worthwhile taking a closer look at the **INSIDER TIP** four bronze sculptures based on characters in popular Norwegian fairy tales by the artist Dyre Vaa. Make a short detour and cross the bridge where you'll find the **INSIDER TIP**

Norwegian Design and Architecture Centre (Mon, Tue, Fri 10am–5pm, Wed/Thu 10am–8pm, Sat/Sun noon–5pm | free entrance | Hausmannsgate 16). The centre is housed in a former transformer station – a good example of how well the industrial landscape along the river has been put to new use. Go back across Anker Bridge to the right bank and continue your walk to **Brenneriveien** where the little

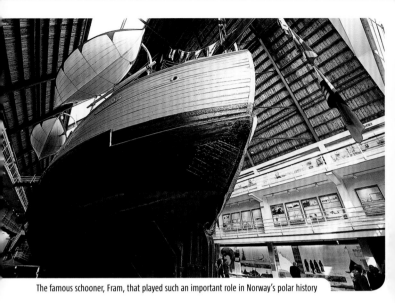
The famous schooner, Fram, that played such an important role in Norway's polar history

river becomes urban and very narrow once again. The well-known jazz bar Blå → p. 69 is on the left bank. On Sundays, cross the footbridge and explore the market held from noon–5pm selling crafts and household items.

The path along the right back will soon bring you to Nedre Foss, the lower waterfall. The river used to be navigable up to this point. The hopper that can be seen from afar is the last remaining testimony to the flour mills that used to flourish. Student flats have now been built here.

A little further on you come to Kuba which can be reached by crossing a wooden bridge over the river. The place did not get its name from the many spontaneous summer parties, political rallies and concerts that give the area its almost Caribbean flair on light summer nights, but from a gasworks that once stood here which had a cube-shaped gasometer.

Walk through the park and up to Åmot suspension bridge, which will take you back to the right bank. It originally stood in Modum to the west of Oslo and has been rebuilt here in Grünerløkka. After a steep climb you will reach Øvre Foss. The upper waterfall is undisputedly the most beautiful on the River Akerselva.

There is a charming little wooded house, the ● INSIDER TIP Hønse Lovisas Hus, right next to the waterfall. The tiny café is an oasis of peace and quiet and makes the best fresh waffles, served with cream and jam, in the whole city area. The red-painted house lies at the centre of what was once an industrialised area along the Akerselva – which included the spinning mills Hjula and Graah and, a few hundred yards further up river, the engineering company Myhren that made the machines for businesses on the Akerselva. At the factory buildings, a detour to the right to Oscar Braatens plass and to INSIDER TIP Vertshus Oscar Braaten (tel. 22 38 17 40 | Budget) can be recommended. If you need some fortification, the through and

through Norwegian menu also includes the hearty hikers' breakfast *torshov-frokost* made with potatoes, eggs and bacon – washed down with a glass of beer.

Just before Nydalen, the path turns away from the river. Nydalen today is a modern district with schools, hotels and its own underground station. Beyond Nydalen you cross back over the river that here is more like a mountain stream. Keep left, then turn right after a short distance heading for Nydal dam where the Akerselva plummets into the valley below. At its foot, a small pond has formed where there is an ● **INSIDER TIP** idyllic place to swim on the far bank. Although you are still within the city boundary it feels like being in the middle of nowhere surrounded by intact countryside. If you come here on a summer's evening, with a bit of luck you may even catch a glimpse of a beaver in the gently flowing water or at least see its lodge.

The Norwegian Museum of Science and Technology *(20 June –20 Aug daily 10am–6pm, otherwise Tue–Fri 9am–4pm, Sat/Sun 11am–6pm | 90 NOK | www.teknisk museum.no)* paints a clear picture of the history of Akerselva's industrialisation and provides an opportunity to relive your impressions from the walk as well as a glimpse of state-of-the-art Norwegian technology so influenced by the oil industry. Opposite the museum, on the other side of the railway track, is Kjelsås station, from where trains (line 54) run every 6 mins. at peak times back to the city centre.

2 EXPLORING THE MUSEUMS ON BYGDØY PENINSULA

Breathe in the fjord air and find out more about Norway's history. The ● Bygdøy Peninsula to the southwest of the centre is an invitation to find out more about the culture of the Norwegian

people and its national heroes – all of whom were at home on the water. It's fitting to start the walk that takes half a day with a boat trip. Bygdøy also boasts some lovely houses, lots of hidden places to go for a swim along the wooded fjord shoreline and a handful of fascinating museums. Take your swimming things and a towel with you. You can't lose your way on Bygdøy and all the sights are well signposted.

A perfect setting: a blue sky and a blue fjord. After a much too short a summer night, the crossing on the **INSIDER TIP** ▶ Bygdøy ferry *(no. 91 from Rathausanleger 3 | April–Oct daily 8.45am–8.45pm | 40 NOK)*, will wake you up like a cold morning shower if you find a place on the narrow deck at the bow. On the grass, just a few yards from the quay, you'll find yourself right in the middle of Norway's proud Arctic history. Roald Amundsen and his crew sailed through the Northwest Passage between 1903 and 1906 in the single-masted ship, Gjøa, a 21m (69ft)-long, round-bellied schooner. The Gjøa is part of the Maritime Museum that is behind it to the left *(mid May–end Aug daily 10am–6pm, otherwise Tue–Fri 10am–3pm, Thu until 6pm, Sat/Sun 10am–4pm | 60 NOK)*. The most important exhibit is the carefully restored *Stokke Boat* from the 2nd century BC – the oldest boat of any kind to be found in Norway. While the Gjøa has to stand in the open, a museum was built for the most famous wooden ship in the world back in 1936. To the right of the maritime museum, Fram can be seen in the larger of the two triangular buildings. Between 1893–1912 the schooner, noted for its extremely broad and bulky hull, sailed the treacherous waters near the North and South Poles. Fridtjof Nansen and his team drifted with the pack ice for three whole years. In 1895 he set off on skis with the meteorologist Hjalmar

Not just traditional costumes and buildings: a day in the Norsk Folkemuseum is undiluted Norway

Johansen for the North Pole. Although this attempt failed, the return journey on board the *Fram* down the coast of Norway in 1896 was a triumphal one. Nansen and his crew had, after all, discovered polar deserts that had previously been unknown and had survived. In 1898 Otto Sverdrup chose the ship for his Greenland expedition and, in 1912, Roald Amundsen headed off in the schooner for the Antarctic and became the first person to reach the South Pole with his dog sleighs. To put it in a nutshell: Norway's glorious polar history made on one single ship *(June–Aug daily 9am–6pm, Sept/March–May daily 10am–5pm, Oct–Feb 10am–3pm | 60 NOK)*.

Half-an-hour outside, perhaps a small bite to eat on the sandy ☼ shore or on the grass is advisable early on – as at lunchtime this part of Bygdøy is heaving with tourists. Take in the view before heading inland for the Kon-Tiki Museum *(June–Aug daily 9.30am–5.30pm, April/May/Sept 10am–5pm, Oct–March 10.30am–4pm | 65 NOK)* dedicated to one of Norway's best-known and most controversial scientists, Thor Heyerdahl. Heyerdahl sailed 4300 nautical miles from South America across the Pacific to Polynesia in his famous balsa tree raft, the *Kon-Tiki*. He took 57 days to complete the stretch between Morocco and Barbados in another boat, the papyrus *Ra II*. Statues from the Easter Islands and a model of the reed boat *Tigris*, with which Heyerdahl sailed from the Tigris and Euphrates across the Indian Ocean to the Horn of Africa, are some of the other most important exhibits in the museum.

Bygdøy is a wealthy area, as a short walk to the west and another few hundred yards along Langviksveien will show you, taking you past some imposing, well-screened private houses set in large, carefully tended gardens. Of particular interest is the ★ Vikingskipshuset, the Viking Ship Museum, in which the Oseberg, Gokstad and Tune ships are displayed.

The three ships from the Viking period were discovered last century on the southeast shore of Oslo Fjord and, together with the other exhibits, provide a clear insight into the death cult, everyday objects, weapons and clothing of the Norwegians' reputedly so warlike ancestors *(June–Aug daily 9am–6pm, Sept–May daily 10am–4pm | 70 NOK)*. You could end your foray into the past here if it were not for the **Norsk Folkemuseum** *(mid May–mid Sept daily 10am–6pm, mid Sept–mid May Mon–Fri 11am–3pm, Sat/Sun 11am–4pm | 100 NOK)*, Norway's largest museum, just a stone's throw away to the north. Let yourself be transported back in time in this open-air museum, which has been laid out by region, and take a look at the construction methods, traditional clothing and crafts of seven centuries. There are more than 150 buildings ranging from stave churches and farmhouses to workshops and town houses, with performances of traditional dances, songs and many other activities. A summer's day spent in the Museum of Cultural History is undiluted Norway and a lot of fun for children too. A regular bus services stops outside all sights on Bygdøy and you never have to wait longer than 10 mins. The journey back to the city centre takes around 20 mins.

3 AROUND HOLMENKOLLEN AND ITS OLYMPIC HISTORY

A visit to Holmenkollen is part and parcel of any trip to Oslo, even in summer. A trip on the most famous stretch of the city's suburban railway network, the most modern ski arena in Europe, the most beautiful views of the capital and the fjord, and a walk in the footsteps of world-famous winter sports men and women, are enough to pack into an full half-day excursion. The suggested route between the two stops is a good 2.5km (1½mi) and is well signposted.

Trains depart from **Majorstuen** (line 1 B a) every 15 mins. For years, this stretch has been known as the 'Holmenkollbanen'. 30 mins. later you alight at **Frognerseter** and, after just a short stroll, you can stop at **Café Seterstua**, Frognerseter famous lodge set in the high summer pastures *(Mon–Sat 11am–10pm, Sun 11am–9pm | Holmenkollenveien 200)*. Take a look at the marvellous dark-stained wooden building with carved pillars, beams and dragon heads from the inside as well, buy a traditional cup of cocoa and a slice of apple cake and settle down on the ⚜ terrace which has a fantastic view over woods, the city and the fjord. You will keep the same panoramic view for a little while if you take the forest path to Holmenkollen to the left of the road. You're now right in the middle of the 1952 **Olympic cross-country trail** – last used by Nordic stars during the 2011 World Championships. It is a gentle walk almost as far as ⚜ **Midtstubakken**, the smaller ski jump, that was also built for 2011. Don't miss out on making this detour – there's no better view than the one from the jump. Then, to the right, cross the Holmenkollenveien road near **Holmenkollen kapell → p. 49**. To the left you'll be heading straight for the **new stadium** and the **biathlon shooting range**. The grandstand is in front of you and, behind, is the massive **new ski jump → p. 48**. With a bit of luck you may be able to see some jumpers during a summer training session and get some impression of what it must be like here during the famous ski jumping event at the beginning of March. Leave the Olympic Grounds with the ski stadium on your right and stroll back down to the Holmenkollen stop where you can catch the train back to the city centre.

TRAVEL WITH KIDS

Like all Scandinavians, the Norwegians are also very child-friendly. Youngsters are always taken seriously and actively involved in things and men and women have equal rights bringing up children. Highchairs are provided as a matter of course in restaurants and many have children's menus too. The city's parks (most of which have playgrounds) are popular meeting places.

INSIDER TIP ▶ SPLASHING AROUND ON OSLO'S ISLANDS (117 F3) (*ⓜ F–H 7–8*)

The larger islands in Oslo Fjord – Hovedøya, Langøyene and Gressholmen – are perfect places to visit in summer. Langøyene and Gressholmen (actually 3 island in all) are particularly suitable for families. The best place to swim is in a nature reserve on Rambergøya, about 10 mins. from the main island of Gressholmen. The ferry (line 93) from Vippetangen quay to the south of Akershus Fortress will take you there in around 15 mins. For departure times, check the timetable (*Ruter* public transport company). There is a large grassy area, a shop and WC next to the long sandy beach at Langøyene. Bathers wanting to go to Langøyene should take the ferry line 94 from Vippetangen. *Island ticket (øy-billetten) adults 40, children 20 NOK*

BOGSTAD GÅRD (117 E2) (*ⓜ 0*)

A municipally-run farm with sheep, cows, horses, chickens and rabbits, organic vegetables and lots of space for children. Adults may want to take a closer look at the grand manorial farmhouse. The guided tours are, unfortunately, only in Norwegian *(Tue–Sun 1pm, 2pm | 60 NOK)*. Plan a whole afternoon for this countryside excursion. *Tue–Sun noon–4pm | free entrance | Sørkedalsveien 826 | www.bogstad.no | tram 2 to Røa, the bus 41 to Sørkedalen*

INSIDER TIP ▶ INTERNASJONAL BARNEKUNSTMUSEUM ● (0) (*ⓜ 0*)

An unusual museum with an unusual aim, namely to collect, conserve and explain children's art from around the globe – and to create new works. This generally takes place in the studio where children can experiment with a variety of different techniques. Dancing, singing and games are also on offer. Adults can join in but don't have much say in things. The museum

Cows, reptiles and children's art: children feel perfectly at home in a country where they are even given their own museum

garden is a little fantasy area where budding artists are allowed to let off steam. *Tue–Thu 9.30am–2pm, Sun 11am–4pm | adults 60, children 40 NOK | Lille Frøens vei 4 | www.barnekunst.no | T-bane 1: Frøen*

REPTILPARK (108 B4) (🅜 J3)

The parrot is called Junior, the crocodile Brutus and the iguana Charlie. They and their more-or-less harmless friends live in Oslo's reptile park. The 'do not touch' signs also apply to the spiders, insects, frogs and snakes which are always fed on Tue at 5pm. *April–Aug daily 10am–6pm | adults 100, children 70 NOK | St. Olavs gate 2 | www. reptilpark.no | bus 37: Nordahl Bruns gate*

TEKNISK MUSEUM (105 E1) (🅜 O)

There's always something of interest going on in the Norwegian Museum of Science, Technology and Medicine – especially for younger visitors. Interactive installations, a robot centre and a planetarium are just some of the highlights. *Tue–Fri 9am–4pm (end June–mid Aug incl. Mon), Sat/Sun 11am–6pm | adults 90, children 50 NOK | Kjelsåsveien 143 | www.tekniskmuseum. no | tram 12 (Kjelsås) or 11 (Disen): Kjelsås*

TUSENFRYD (117 F4) (🅜 O)

Norway's largest fun park is approx. 20km (12½mi) south of Oslo and has 33 different and sometimes neck-breaking attractions – from the gently turning merry-go-round to a speedy whiz on northern Europe's largest big-dipper – the *Thunder Coaster*, or the *Super Splash* that ends up in the water. *July–Aug daily 10.30am–7pm, otherwise times vary greatly | day pass – under 95cm: free, under 120cm: 270 NOK, over 120cm: 345 NOK | www.tusenfryd.no | E 18 southbound, exit Vinterbro, then signposted; bus during opening hours every 30 mins., adults 40, children 25 NOK*

FESTIVALS & EVENTS

PUBLIC HOLIDAYS

1 Jan *New Year's Day*; **1 May** *Labour Day*; **Maundy Thursday**; **Easter Monday**; **17 May** *Constitution Day*; **Ascension**; **Whit Monday**; **24 Dec** *Christmas Eve (half day)*; **25/26 Dec** *Christmas*

FESTIVALS & EVENTS

JANUARY/FEBRUARY

▶ *Oslo Vinternattfestival:* chamber music on the last weekend in Jan or the first in Feb in churches, cafés and the old Oslo Lodge. *www.detnorskekammerorkester.no*

FEBRUARY

The ▶ INSIDER TIP ▶ *Rockfestival by:larm* featuring some 50 mostly young groups is very Nordic in character. Participants are selected by a jury; the standard is astonishingly high.

MARCH

The ▶ ★ *Holmenkollen Sunday* (usually the 2nd in the month) is more than just ski jumping. The public festival starts in the underground and there is a brilliant atmosphere around the jump whatever the weather, fuelled by excellent jumps, punch and grilled sausages.

APRIL

At the ▶ *Inferno Metal Festival* 40 bands and fans of really heavy music party to excess for 4 days. *www.infernofestival.net*

MAY

The highlight of the national holiday on 17 May is the ▶ *children's parade* along Karl Johans gate to the palace square, passing the royal family. The rest of the day is party time too – in every district, in all the parks and always with and for children.

JUNE

▶ ★ ● *Midsummer's night:* All Oslo celebrates the shortest night of the year on 23 June with campfires and lots of alcohol in the open, especially in Frogner Park.
▶ *Norwegian Wood:* Oslo's oldest and most famous rock festival at *Frognerbadet* with international classic rock and Norwegian groups. *www.norwegianwood.no* / *tickets from Billettservice, at post offices or Narvesen and 7-Eleven outlets*

Culture *sans frontières*: Oslo's events calendar features many renowned and international stars especially in the field of music

AUGUST

▶ **Øyafestivalen** international rock festival early in the month in *Middelalderparken*. www.oyafestivalen.com

▶ **Oslo Kammermusikkfestival** with top string quartets from around the world. An appealing mixture, a relaxed atmosphere and unusual venues such as the courtyard in Akershus Fortress. *www.oslokammer musikkfestival.no*

AUGUST/SEPTEMBER

▶ **Ibsen Festival:** First-class theatre get-together with performances of works by the Norwegian playwright by international ensembles. *www.ibsenfestivalen. no | tickets: tel. 8150 08 11*

OCTOBER

▶ **CODA Oslo International Dance Festival:** Top-notch dance theatre with guests from around the world in the new opera house and Dansens Hus. *www.codadance-fest.no*

▶ **Film fra Sør:** A potpourri of delights for cinema fans with feature films and documentaries, esp. from Asia, Africa and South America. Associated musical events and meetings for anything to do with non-Hollywood films. *www.filmfrasor.no/en*

NOVEMBER

▶ **INSIDER TIP** ▶ **Oslo World Music Festival:** A highlight in Oslo's music year in the first full week with more than 20 concerts with musicians from around the globe. *www. rikskonsertene.no/osloworldmusicfestival*

DECEMBER

▶ **Concert on the occasion of the Nobel Peace Prize** on 11 Dec in the *Oslo Spektrum* concert hall attended by the recipient of the award. *Tickets via Billettservice (tel. 81 53 31 33 | www.billettservice.no).*

LINKS, BLOGS, APPS & MORE

LINKS

▶ goscandinavia.about.com/od/cityprofileoslo/p/huboslo.htm Useful information for tourists on what to see and where to stay as well as links to updates on the weather, public transport, history, events and much more

▶ www.visitoslo.com/en Official travel guide to Oslo. Very easy to navigate despite the mass of information. Apart from information and deals for the tourism and travel industry, there are also tips for congresses and conferences. Photos, videos and personal tips can also be uploaded here after your holiday

▶ www.airbnb.com/oslo Wide range of accommodation in Oslo – rooms and flats – posted on this site with guest ratings and comments by the hosts

▶ www.norway.org.uk (US site: www.norway.org) Norway's official website with information on planning a trip to Norway, embassy and consulate details, tips for studying or working there, as well as facts and figures about the country, its culture and history

BLOGS & FORUMS

▶ norglish.wordpress.com This blog by a 25-year-old English lass, relatively new to the city, will put anyone in a good mood. Very personal and entertaining, touching on such varied subjects as Norwegian patriotism and Dennis Hopper

▶ wikitravel.org/en/Oslo Not just a lot of information but a place for you to write something for the travel guide in Wikipedia format after your holiday

▶ oslostil.blogspot.com For all fashionistas and those who want to become one. Lots of inspirational ideas on how to expand your wardrobe and improve on your personal style of dress

Regardless of whether you are still preparing your trip or already in Oslo: these addresses will provide you with more information, videos and networks to make your holiday even more enjoyable

▶ www.youtube.com/watch?v=XZQNoV2ynrQ Short video exploring one of Europe's smallest and most welcoming capitals. Professional commentary of many interesting sites

▶ http://vimeo.com/22301511 Artistically shot impressions of the city in slow motion set to up-beat music – dreamy and stylish – rather like the city itself

▶ www.youtube.com/watch?v=Flop3kYBiYc A typical holiday clip of Oslo in winter from arriving at the airport to many of the sights and a few private glimpses into the life of a hobby videomaker

VIDEOS, STREAMS & PODCASTS

▶ City Guide Oslo from APlus Software Using this app you don't need to be online to find your way around or check historical and cultural facts. Safety tips and fun facts also included

▶ AllSubway Timetables of public transport systems in more than 120 cities – including Oslo of course

▶ Radio 1-App This free app lets you tune into Oslo Radio 1 as well as local stations in Bergen, Trondheim and Stavanger if you plan to travel around the country. Internet access needed for the live stream

▶ Oslo (Norway) Map Offline This provides an extremely useful map of the city of Oslo that can also be used offline

APPS

▶ www.tripwolf.com/en/guide/show/6841/Norway/Oslo The 'gateway to the north' is introduced by the travel community with all its varied and fascinating facets. Tips on where to go in the evening and which restaurants to head for, along with lots of photos

▶ www.dopplr.com/place/no/oslo Lots of interesting things to be found here too, posted by people who have been to Oslo. Tips for family-friendly places to stay, to yoga schools and the best markets in the city

NETWORK

TRAVEL TIPS

ARRIVAL

✈ A number of different airlines offer regular flights from the UK to Oslo. British Ariways (www.britishairways.com) and SAS (www.flysas.com), as well as the no-frills airlines Norwegian Air Shuttle (www.norwegian.com) and Ryanair (www.ryanair.com) among others, fly out of various British airports to the Norwegian capital. The main airport, Gardemoen International, is 40km (25mi) to the north of Oslo and benefits from a fast train service (one way: 180 NOK). Torp/Sandefjord is more than 100km (60mi) to the west, Rygge (misleadingly also known as Oslo Airport) is 70km (44mi) to the south east of Oslo. Both are connected to the capital by a bus service – Torp–Oslo takes at least 1½ hours and costs 220 NOK (return: 290 NOK); Rygge–Oslo costs 120 NOK (return: 210 NOK). Flights to and from the USA and Canada go via Copenhagen, Stockholm or other major European airports.

🚗 The last car ferry route between the UK and Norway (Newcastle to Bergen) was withdrawn in September 2008. However several ferries operate between Norway and mainland Europe (e.g. to Denmark; www.norwaydirect.com). Most operators offer package deals for a car and passengers, and most lines offer concessions. An additional charge is normally made for bicycles and boats.

🚆 Travelling from London to Norway by train is possible but takes a long time. If you take a lunchtime Eurostar to Brussels, a connecting high-speed train to Cologne, the overnight train to Copenhagen and connecting trains to Oslo, you arrive in the evening the day after leaving London. An InterRail Pass can be recommended for a trip to Scandinavia (www.interrailnet.com). The main station (Oslo S) is in the city centre. All trams and underground lines stop here.

RESPONSIBLE TRAVEL

It doesn't take a lot to be environmentally friendly whilst travelling. Don't just think about your carbon footprint whilst flying to and from your holiday destination but also about how you can protect nature and culture abroad. As a tourist it is especially important to respect nature, look out for local products, cycle instead of driving, save water and much more. If you would like to find out more about eco-tourism please visit: www.ecotourism.org

BANKS & CREDIT CARDS

You can pay with a Visacard or Mastercard everywhere; with American Express almost everywhere. Cash dispensers (minibank) can be found on almost every street corner and take all standard international credit cards and EC card. Money can be exchanged free of charge at the five Oslo branches of the Swedish Forex Bank (two at the main station as well as at Brugata 8, Egertorget and Fridtjof Nansens plass 6 | opening times under www.forex.no/Om-FOREX/Apningstider). Between 15 May–15 Aug banks are only open Mon–Fri 9am–2.30pm, otherwise Mon–Fri 9am–3.30pm, Thu 5pm.

From arrival to weather

Holiday from start to finish: the most important addresses and information for your Oslo trip

CUSTOMS

1 litre of spirits, 1.5 litres of wine and 2 litres of beer may be imported into Norway as well as 200 cigarettes and cash up to a value of 25,000 NOK. The following articles can be imported tax-free into the EU: 200 cigarettes or 50 cigars or 250 grams of tobacco, 1 litre of spirits 2 litres of wine, as well as goods to the value of 2500 NOK. For more information see: *www.hmrc.gov.uk/customs/ arriving/arrivingnoneu.htm*

Travellers to the United States who are returning residents of the country do not have to pay duty on articles purchased overseas up to the value of $800, but there are limits on the amount of alcoholic beverages and tobacco products. For the regulations for international travel for U.S. residents please see *www.cbp.gov*

CYCLING

There are few cycle paths in the city centre. Two main cycle axes running north–south and east–west through Oslo are being planned. Until then, if you want to be able to enjoy your cycling trip, you should use the hiking paths around the edge of the city which are excellent for day excursions. Detailed cycle maps for the east and west of the city are available from *Syklistenes Landsforening (Postboks 88 83 | Youngstorget | 0028 Oslo | post@syklistene.no | office: Storgate 3, 2nd floor).*

You can only hire bikes at *Ski & Guide* near Holmenkollen *(rate per day: 350 NOK | Tryvannsveien 61 | www.ski-guide.no | T-bane 1: Voksenkollen)* or in the depths of Oslo's forests at the *DNT* cabin *Kikut (see: www.kikutstua.no).*

Relaxing on Oslo Fjord

EMBASSIES & CONSULATES

BRITISH EMBASSY
Thomas Heftyes gate 8, 0264 Oslo, tel.: +47 23 13 27 00, www.ukinnorway.fco.gov. uk/en

EMBASSY OF THE UNITED STATES
Henrik Ibsens gate 48, 0244 Oslo, switchboard: +47 21 30 85 40, norway.usembassy. gov

EMBASSY OF CANADA
Wergelandsveien 7 (4th floor), 0244 Oslo, +47 22 99 53 00, www.canadainternational. gc.ca/norway

EMERGENCY SERVICES

Fire brigade *tel. 110;* police *tel. 112;* ambulance *tel. 113.*

EVENTS & ADVANCE SALES

www.visitoslo.com/en has a comprehensive events calendar. The free bi-monthly magazine *What's on Oslo* (in English) is

available at tourist information offices and in most hotels. Tickets can be booked in advance online under *www.billettservice. no*, otherwise tickets can only be bought at the respective ticket office on the evening of the event.

GUIDED TOURS & SIGHTSEEING TOURS

The *Grand tour of Oslo* by bus and boat may be a bit pricey at 640 NOK but you really do see a lot *(end May–end Aug daily 10.30am–6pm | leaves from quay 3 opposite the city hall | reservations: tel. 23 35 68 90)*. The tour takes in all the most important highlights in the city and the most important museums. The highlight is the 2-hour boat trip including a prawn buffet *(incl. in price)*. HMK sightseeing buses depart from the west of the city hall every day in summer *(duration: 2–5 hrs. |*

dep. 10.15am | 225–365 NOK | reservation under www.hmk.no/booking, in your hotel or at a tourist information office).
Hop-on hop-off tours on a small ship on Oslo Fjord are always good and last 1½ hrs. *(3 stops | four departures daily, the first at 9.45am, the last at 2.15pm, July/ Aug until 7pm | from quay 3 opposite the city hall | NOK 175)*. Discounts available for all tours for holders of an Oslo Pass.

HEALTH

For the emergency doctor and ambulance service tel. 113. *Oslo Legevakt* hospital is open 24-hours a day *(Storgata 40 | tel. 22 93 22 93)*. A European Health Insurance Card (EHIC) is advisable. A percentage of the costs however has to be paid by the patient – depending on the treatment 130–220 NOK, x-ray: 200 NOK. The only chemist in Oslo open 24-hours is on

BOOKS & FILMS

▶ **Lillelord** – Written by Johan Borgen, Norway's most distinguished modern novelist, and set in turn-of-the-century Oslo. Lillelord is the impeccably behaved ''good boy' of a comfortable family who is seen in a more sinister light by his teachers and the children on Oslo's streets.

▶ **Norwegian detective stories** – Norwegian crime writers have enjoyed a wide international readership for many years now. The series of books about the alcoholic detective Harry Hole by Jo Nesbø focuses on the darker side of life in the Norwegian capital, as does Anne Holt's police officer Hanne Willemsen.

Oslo is also at the centre of the crime novels written by Karin Fossum and Unni Lindell.

▶ **Uno** – The raw reality of Oslo's criminal milieu poignantly captured in this award-winning film (2004) by the young Norwegian director Aksel Hennie (DVD with English subtitles).

▶ **Hawaii Oslo** – A Norwegian drama film directed by Erik Poppe (2004) about Vidar who is haunted by dreams that turn out to be true. Excellent screenplay and a slow-moving narrative (DVD with English subtitles).

the square outside the main station (*Jernbanetorget*).

INTERNET CAFÉS & WI-FI

Wi-Fi is available virtually everywhere in Oslo. Internet access is available for visitors in every hotel foyer and almost every café and bar. As a result, there are not many internet cafés. A large commercial net point is *Haugen nettkafé* (115 C–D2) (*ф K4*) at the central bus station (*Busterminalen, Schweigaardsgate 6*). You can surf for free in libraries.

NEWSPAPERS

English papers are available at the main station and in kiosks in the city centre such as on the Karl Johans gate and at *Nationaltheatret* station.

OPENING TIMES

Supermarkets are open on weekdays from 9am–9pm, some until 11pm. Sat 9am–4pm or 6pm. Most other shops are open Mon–Fri 9am–8pm, Sat 4pm.

ORGANIC FOOD

Food sourced from organic producers, such as through the international Demeter organisation, are available in 4 Oslo branches of *Helios*. The best selection of shops is in Grünerløkka (*Storgata 53 A*) (108 C5) (*ф K4*) and Smalgangen (109 D6) (*ф K4*). The chain *Life*, that has some 20 branches in Oslo, also stocks many organic products. You will find *Fairtrade Max Havelaar* products (incl. coffee, fruit, juice and wine) in supermarkets which have a more extensive range of products. All organic produce in Norway is certified by the internationally recognised organisation *Debio*.

BUDGETING

Taxi	from £9.50/$15 *for a short trip*
Cappuccino	from £2.50/$3.80 *a cup*
Souvenirs	approx. £19/$30 *for a wooden beaker*
Beer	£4.50–6.50/$7.50–10 *for a ½L glass of draught beer*
Hot dog	£2.50/$3.80 *for a grilled or boiled hot dog*
CD	approx. £15/$23 *for a Norwegian jazz CD*

OSLO PASS

Free entrance to more than 30 museums and municipal swimming pools, free use of public transport and free parking in pay-and-display car parks are good reasons for visitors to buy an Oslo Pass for 1, 2 or 3 days. Another plus point: 20–30% discounts on popular city tours, discounts at certain car hire companies and in many restaurants. The Oslo Pass is available at tourist information offices. Price: 3 days 420 (children 160 NOK), 2 days 340 (children 120 NOK) and 1 day 230 (children 100 NOK).

PARKING

There is virtually no free parking in the city centre. Municipal car parks charge from Mon–Fri 9am–6pm, Sat 9am–3pm. Note that there is a maximum stay of 3 hours on many car parks. This also applies to Oslo Pass holders who are otherwise allowed to park here free of charge. The many multi-storey car parks in the city on the other hand are expensive but safe and

there is no max. stay. Virtually all hotels have their own parking spaces for guests.

PHONES & MOBILE PHONES

Country codes from Norway are *0044* (UK), *001* (US and Canada), *00353* (Ireland), *0061* (Australia), *0064* (New Zealand) and *0027* (South Africa). The international country code for Norway from abroad is *0047*. All telephone numbers in Norway (except for special nos.) have 8 digits. Mobile phone nos. start with 9 or 4. GSM mobile phone users can telephone from anywhere in Norway without any problem. The few telephone boxes still left take coins or cards (available from kiosks).

POST

Post offices are open Mon–Fri 8am–5pm and Sat 9am–3pm. Many food shops also have a post office counter *(post i butikk)*, recognisable by the red post office logo *(posten)*.

PRICES

If you plan your visit well, you can save a lot of money in one of the most expensive capitals in the world. The price of a hotel room always includes a generous breakfast that can make lunch unnecessary. There are virtually no cheap supermarkets in the city centre so stock up on the edge of town. That makes snacks between meals

WEATHER IN OSLO

	Jan	Feb	March	April	May	June	July	Aug	Sept	Oct	Nov	Dec
Daytime temperatures in °C/°F	−2/28	−1/30	4/39	10/50	16/61	20/68	22/72	21/70	16/61	9/48	3/37	0/32
Nighttime temperatures in °C/°F	−7/19	−7/19	−4/25	1/34	6/43	10/50	13/55	12/54	8/46	3/37	−1/30	−4/25
Sunshine hours/day	2	3	4	6	7	8	7	7	5	3	1	1
Precipitation days/month	8	7	5	7	7	10	11	11	10	10	12	10
Water temperature in °C/°F	3/37	2/36	3/37	5/41	9/48	13/55	16/61	17/63	15/59	11/52	7/45	5/41

and a drink in the pub unnecessary – both of which are incredibly expensive in Oslo.

PUBLIC TRANSPORT

The capital is served by an underground system *(T-bane)*, 6 tram lines *(trikk)*, ferry connections to islands in Oslo Fjord and buses. Single tickets (incl. those for the *T-bane*) can be bought in buses and trams *(40 NOK)* and are valid for 1 hour. Tickets bought at a kiosk near the stop/station or at a ticket office are considerably cheaper *(27 NOK)*. Holders of an Oslo Pass can travel free on all public transport services. Timetables are available under *www.trafi kanten.no* to help plan local trips.

TAXI

The 3 taxi companies with switchboards are *Norgestaxi (tel. 0 80 00)*, *Oslo Taxi (tel. 0 23 23)* and *Taxi 2 (tel. 80 08 29 42)*. Taxis have taximeters. The price per km is around 35 NOK *(city centre–Bygdøy approx. 180 NOK)*. Taxi stands are clearly marked. There are long queues for taxis at weekends from 11pm until the early hours.

TIPPING

Not a matter of course, but if the food and service were good, up to 10% is certainly normal.

TOLLS

A 25 NOK toll is electronically charged to all vehicles entering Oslo along one of the European Routes. No cash payments are possible. Vehicles without an AutoPASS On-Board Unit (OBU) – a tag – on the windscreen are generally sent a bill by post. Anyone staying longer in Norway can buy a tag online by credit card under *www.autopass.no*, e.g. 300 NOK.

CURRENCY CONVERTER

£	NOK	NOK	£
10	89	100	11.25
20	178	200	22.50
30	267	300	33.75
40	356	400	45
50	445	500	56.25
60	534	600	67.50
70	623	700	78.75
80	712	800	90
90	801	900	101.25

$	NOK	NOK	$
10	59	100	17
20	118	200	34
30	177	300	51
40	236	400	68
50	295	500	85
60	354	600	102
70	413	700	119
80	472	800	136
90	531	900	153

For current exchange rates see www.xe.com

TOURIST INFORMATION

www.visitoslo.com/en and *www.visit norway.com* provide useful information to help you plan your visit. *www.senorge. no* keeps you up to date on the weather.

VISITOSLO TOURIST INFORMATION TRAFIKANTEN

Information on transport services at the main station (114 B2) *(ɯ J4)* | *Jernbane-torget 1* | *tel. 81 53 05 55*
At the city hall (113 E1) *(ɯ H4)* | *Fridtjof Nansens plass 5*
At the cruise liner dock near Akershusfestung (113 E3) *(ɯ H5)* | *open in summer when ships come in*

USEFUL PHRASES NORWEGIAN

PRONUNCIATION

In this guide to phrases in the main Norwegian language, *bokmål*, simplified assistance in pronouncing the words has been added in square brackets. Note also that the vowel marked 'ü' in the pronunciation guide is spoken as 'ee' with rounded lips, like the 'u' in French 'tu', -e at the end of a word is a syllable spoken like the 'e' in 'the', and 'g' is pronounced as in 'get'.

IN BRIEF

Yes/No/Maybe	Ja/Nei/Kanskje [ya/nayi/kansh-e]
Please	Vær så snill [vair sho snill]
Thank you	Takk [tak]
Excuse me, please/ Pardon?	Unnskyld [ünnshüll]/Hva sa du? [va sa dü]
May I ...?/	Kan jeg ...? [kann yayi]
I would like to .../	Jeg vil gjerne ... [yayi vill yern-e]/
Have you got ...?	Har du (noen) ... ? [har dü (nuen)]
How much is ...	Hva koster ... ? [va koster]
I (don't) like that	Det liker jeg (ikke) [de leeker yayi [ick-e]]
good/bad/broken/	bra [bra]/dårlig [dorli]/ødelagt [erdelagt]/
doesn't work	fungerer ikke [fungerer ick-e]
too much/much/little	for mye [for mü-e]/mye [mü-e]/lite [leet-e]
all/nothing	alt [alt]/ingenting [ingenting]
Help!/Attention!/	Hjelp! [yelp]/Pass på! [pass po]/
Caution!	Forsiktig! [forzikti]
ambulance/police/fire brigade	sykebil [zük-e-beel]/politi [politi]/
	brannvesen [brannvayzen]
prohibition/forbidden	Forbud/forbudt [forbütt]
danger/dangerous	Fare [far-e]/farlig [farli]

GREETINGS, FAREWELL

Good morning!/afternoon/	God morgen! [gu morn]/God dag! [gu dag]/
Hello!	Hei! [high]
Good evening!/night!	God kveld! [gu kvell]/God natt! [gu natt]
goodbye!/See you	Ha det! [ha de]
My name is ...	Jeg heter ... [yayi hayter]
What's your name?	Hva heter du? [va hayter dü]
I'm from ...	Jeg er fra ... [yayi er fra]

Snakker du norsk?

"Do you speak Norwegian?" This guide will help you to say the basic words and phrases in Norwegian

DATE AND TIME

Monday/Tuesday	mandag [mandag]/tirsdag [teersdag]
Wednesday/Thursday	onsdag [unsdag]/torsdag [toorsdag]
Friday/Saturday	fredag[fraydag]/lørdag [lerdag]
Sunday/working day	søndag [zerndag]/ukedag[ük-edag]
holiday	helligdag [helligdag]
today/tomorrow/yesterday	i dag [ee dag]/i morgen [ee morn]/i går [ee gor]
hour/minute	time [teem-e]/minutt [minütt]
day/night/week	dag [dag]/natt[natt]/uke [ük-e]
month/year	måned [mon-ed]/år [oar]
What time is it?	Hva er klokken? [va air klocken?]
It's three o'clock/	Klokken er tre [klocken air tre]/
It's half past three	Klokken er halv fire [klocken air hal feer-e]

TRAVEL

open/closed	åpent [opent]/stengt [stengt]
entrance/vehicle entrance	inngang [ingang]/innkjørsel [inkyersel]
exit/vehicle exit	utgang [ütgang]/utkjørsel [ütkyersel]
departure/arrival	avgang [avgang]/ankomst [ankommst]
toilets	toaletter [twaletter]
Where is ...?/Where are ...?	Hvor er ...? [voor air]
left/right	venstre [venstr-e]/høyre [her-ir-e]
straight ahead/back	rett fram [rett fram]/tilbake [tillbaak-e]
close/far	nært [nairt]/langt (unna) [langt (ünna)]
bus/tram	buss [büss]/trikk [trick]
underground/taxi/cab	T-bane [te-baan-e]/drosje [drosh-e]
stop/cab stand	stoppested [stopp-e-sted]/
	drosjeholdeplass [drosh-e-holleplass]
parking lot/	parkeringsplass [parkeringsplass]/
parking garage	parkeringshus[parkeringshüss]
street map/map	bykart [bükart]/kart [kart]
train station/	jernbanestasjon [yernbaan-e-stashon]/
harbour/airport	havn [haavn]/flyplass [flüplass]
ticket/supplement	billett [beelett]/påslag [poshlag]
single/return	enkel [enkel]/tur-retur [tür-retür]
train/track/platform	tog [tog]/spor [spoor]/rute [rüt-e]
I would like to rent ...	Jeg vil gjerne leie ... [yayi vill yern-e ly-e]
a car/a bicycle/a boat	en bil [en beel]/sykkel [zükkel]/båt [boat]
petrol/gas station	bensinstasjon [benzinstashon]
breakdown/repair shop	skade/verksted [shaad-e/vairksted]

FOOD & DRINK

Could you please book a table for tonight for four?	Vi vil gjerne bestille et bord for fire personer til i kveld. [vee vill yairn-e bestill-e et boor for feer-e perzooner till ee kvell]
The menu, please	Kan jeg få menyen? [kann yayi fo menü-en]
Could I please have ...?	Kunne jeg få ... ? [künn-e yayi fo]
salt/pepper/sugar	salt [zalt]/pepper [pepper]/sukker [zucker]
vinegar/oil	eddik [eddick]/olje [uly-e]
milk/cream/lemon	melk [melk]/fløte [flert-e]/sitron [zitroon]
with/without ice	med [may]/uten is [üten eess]
vegetarian/allergy	vegetarianer [vegetarianer]/allergi [allergee]
May I have the bill, please?	Jeg vil gjerne betale [yayi vill yairn-e betal-e]

SHOPPING

I'd like .../	Jeg vil gjerne ... [yayi vill yairn-e]/
I'm looking for ...	Jeg leter etter ... [yayi layter etter]
pharmacy/chemist	apotek/parfymeri [apotayk/parfümeree]
baker/market	bakeri [backeree]/torget [torg]
shopping centre/	handlesenter [hand-le-zenter]/
department store	varehus [var-e-hüs]
supermarket	supermarked [süpermark-ed]
more/less	mer [mair]/mindre [mindr-e]
organically grown	biologisk dyrket [bioologish dürket]

ACCOMMODATION

I have booked a room	Jeg har bestilt et rom [yai har bestilt ett room]
single room	enkeltrom [enkeltroom]
double room	dobbeltrom [dobbeltroom]
breakfast/half board/	frokost [frookost]/halvpensjon [halpanshon]/
full board (American plan)	fullpensjon [füllpanshon]
the front/	mot framsiden [moot frammzeeden]/
seafront/	mot sjøen [moot shern]/
lakefront	mot innsjøen [moot innshern]
key/room card	nøkkel/nøkkelkort [nerckel/nerckelkoort]
luggage/suitcase/	bagasje [bagash-e]/koffert [kooffert]/
bag	veske [vesk-e]/bag [beg]

BANKS, MONEY & CREDIT CARDS

bank/ATM	bank [bank]/minibank [minibank]
pin code	bankkode [bankkood-e]
I'd like to change ...	Jeg vil gjerne veksle ... [yayi vill yairn-e vek-sle ...]

cash/credit card	kontant [kontant]/kredittkort [kreditkoort]
bill/coin	seddel [zeddel]/mynt [münt]

HEALTH

doctor/dentist/ paediatrician	lege [legg-e]/tannlege [tannlegg-e]/ barnelege [baan-e-legg-e]
hospital/emergency clinic	sykehus [sük-e-hüs/legevakt [legg-e-vakt]
fever/pain	feber [fayber]/smerter [smairter]
diarrhoea/nausea	diaré [deearay]/kvalme [kvalm-e]
pain reliever/ tablet	smertestillende [smairt-e-stillend-e]/ tablett [tablett]

POST, TELECOMMUNICATIONS & MEDIA

stamp/postcard	frimerke [freemairk-e]/postkort [postkort]
I need a landline phone card/ prepaid card for my -mobile	Jeg trenger et telefonkort/kontantkort [yayi trenger ett telefonkort/kontantkort]
Where can I find internet access?	Hvor er nærmeste internetttilgang? [voor er nairmest-e internetttilgang]
Do I need a special area code?	Må jeg slå et spesielt nummer først? [mo yayi shlo ett speseelt nummer ferst]
dial/	slå et nummer [shlo ett nummer]/
connection/engaged	linje [liny-e]/opptatt [upptatt]
internet connection/wifi	internettilkobling [internett-tilkoblin]

LEISURE, SPORTS & BEACH

(rescue) hut/avalanche	hytte [hütt-e]/ras [raz]
cable car/chair lift	taubane [towbaan-e]/stolheis [stoolhice]
low tide/high tide/ current	fjære [fyair-e]/flo [floo]/ strøm [strerm]
beach/bathing beach	strand [stran]/sjøbad [sherbad]

NUMBERS

0	null [nüll]	10	ti [tee]
1	en [ayn]	11	elleve [ellv-e]
2	to [too]	12	tolv [toll]
3	tre [tre]	20	tjue/tyve [chü-e/tü-ve]
4	fire [feer-e]	100	hundre [hün-dre]
5	fem [fem]	200	tohundre [toohün-dre]
6	seks [zeks]	1000	ettusen [ettüsen]
7	sju/syv [shü/züv]	2000	totusen [tootüsen]
8	åtte [ott-e]	½	en halv [ayn hal]
9	ni [nee]	¼	en kvart [ayn kvart]

NOTES

STREET ATLAS

Green lines [____] indicate Walking tours (p. 78–83)

All tours are also marked on the pull-out map

Photo: Historical buildings in Grünerløkka

Exploring Oslo

The map on the back cover shows how the area has been sub-divided

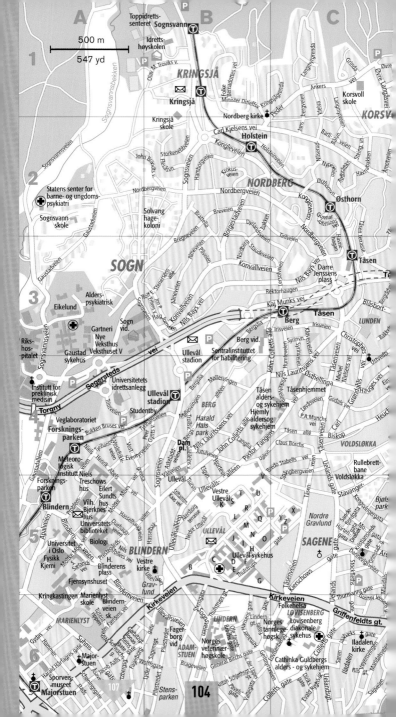

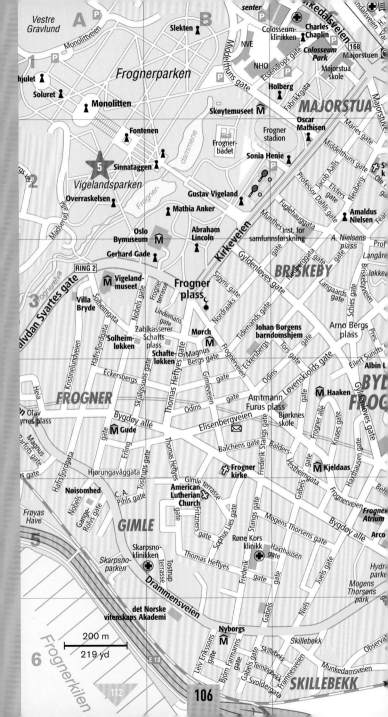

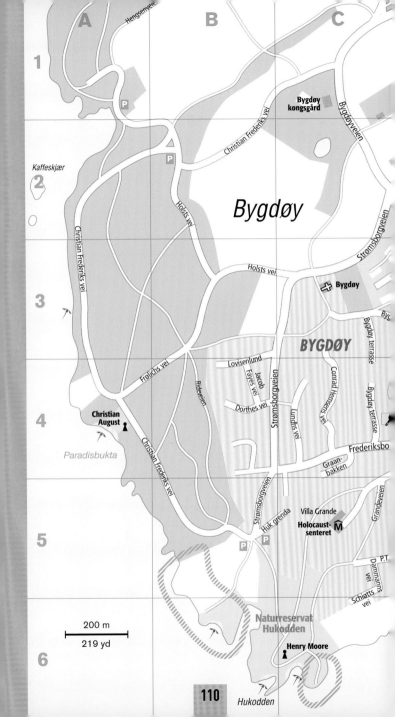

A

B

C

1

Hengsenveien

Christian Frederiks vei

Bygdøveien

Bygdøy kongsgård

P

P

Kaffeskjær

2

Bygdøy

Christian Frederiks vei

Holsts vei

3

Holsts vei

Bygdøy

BYGDØY

Strømsborgveien

Bygdøy terrasse

Bygdøy terrasse

Lovisenlund

Frølichs vei

Jacob Fayes vei

Contrad Hemsens vei

4

Christian August

Rideveien

Dorthes vei

Strømsborgveien

Lunds vei

Frederiksbo

Paradisbukta

Christian Frederiks vei

Graan-bakken

Grandveien

5

Strømsborgveien

Huk grenda

Villa Grande

Holocaust-senteret M̂

P

P

P.T.

Dammanns vei

Schiøtts vei

200 m

219 yd

Naturreservat Hukodden

6

Henry Moore

Hukodden

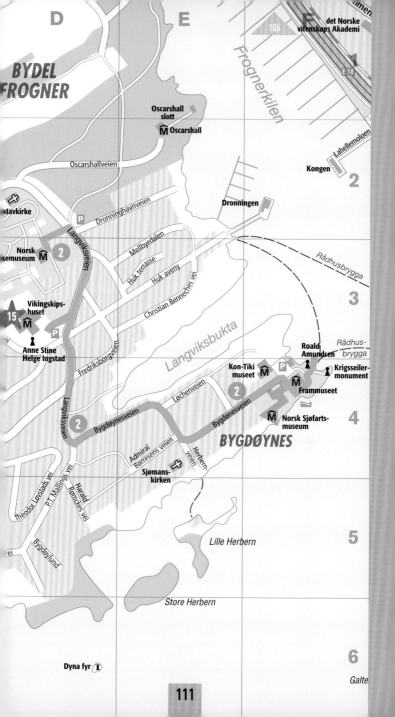

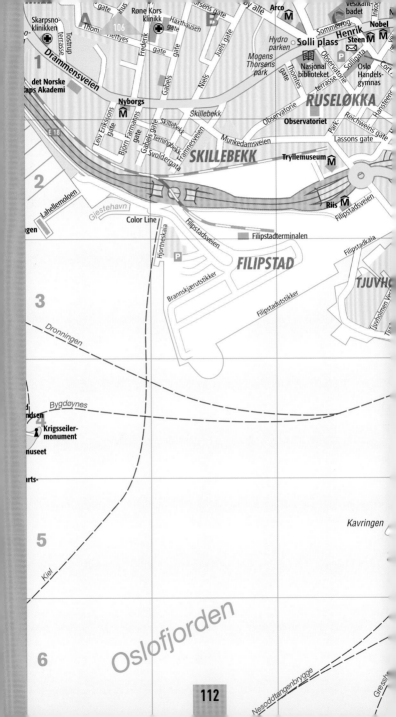

Skarpsno-
klinikken
Testrup
terrasse

det Norske
taps Akademi

Drammensveien

E 18

Nyborgs

Leiv Eriksons gate

Bjørn Farmanns gate

Gabels gate

Skillebekk

Svoldergata

Temingbekk

Framnesveien

Skillebekk

Thom

106

Hertyes

Frederik
gate

Gabels
gate

Niels

Juels gate

Røne Kors
klinikk

Haxthausen
gate

Arco

orsens gate

oy alle

Hydro
parken

Mogens
Thorsens
park

Solli plass

Thorntes
gate

**Nasjonal
biblioteket**

Observatorie
terrasse

Observatorie

**Henrik
Steen**

Sommerrog.

Sollngata

Nobel

**Oslo
Handels-
gymnas**

RUSELØKKA

Reichweins gate

Hansteen

Observatoriet

Munkedamsveien

Lassons gate

SKILLEBEKK

Tryllemuseum

Park-

Riis

Lahellemoloen

Gjestehavn

Color Line

Hjorneskaia

P

Filipstadsveien

Filipstadterminalen

Filipstadsveien

Filipstadkaia

FILIPSTAD

Brannskjærutstikker

Filipstadutstikker

TJUVH

Tjuvholmen Ve

Dronningen

Bygdøynes

d
ndsen

**Krigsseiler-
monument**

nuseet

arts-

Kavringen

Kiel

Oslofjorden

Nesoddtangenbrygge

Gressho

Ibsens gate
Ibsenmuseet
Cora Sandels fødested
Nationaltheatret
Johanne Dybwards plassen
7. Juni plassen
Universitetsplassen i Oslo
Det Norske
National theatret
Dizzie
Paleet Scene West
Oslo Nye Theater
Chat Noir
Karl Johans gate
Konsert-huset
Stenersen-museet
VIKA
Klingenberggata
Stortingsgata
Eidsvolls plass
Stortinget
Wessels plass
Stortinget
Steen & Strøm
Vikatorvet
RING 1
Dr. Mauds gate
Fridtjof Nansens plass
Olav V Kronpr Märthas plass
Frimurer-losjen
Prinsens gate
Musikk-teatret
Nobels Fredssenter
Rådhuset
Rolf Strangers plass
Christiania torv
Åflaskemuseet (Mini Bottle Gallery)
Latter
Rådhus-plassen
Kontraskjæret
Christiania bymodell
Teatermuseet
Gamle Raadhus
Arkitekturmuseet

AKER BRYGGE

Pipervika
Skarpenords-kruttårn
Havnepolitiet
Museet for samtidskunst
Fengsels-museet
Grev Wedels plass
Akershus-utstikker
Hjemme-frontmuseet
Akershus-festning
Knutstårnet
Akershus slott
Fengsels-kirken
Gamle Logen
Oslo Cruise Terminal
Munke-tårnet
Nasjonal-monumentet
Festnings-plassen
Arsenalet
Otto Ruge
Forsvars-museet

200 m
219 yd

Fiskehallen

Utstikker 3
Utstikker 2

Lavettbygningen

Hovedøya

Ruin av cistercienserkloster

113

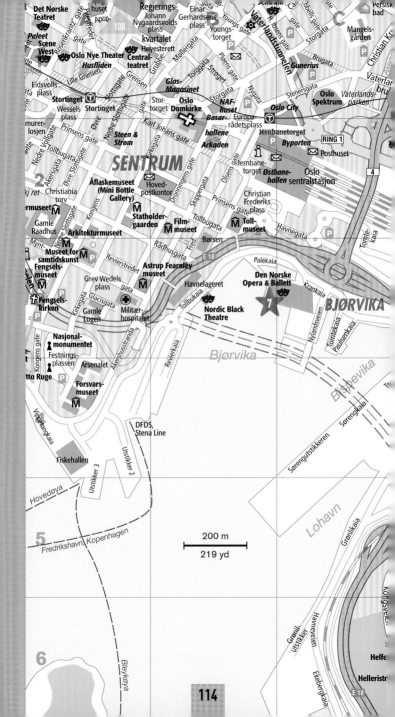

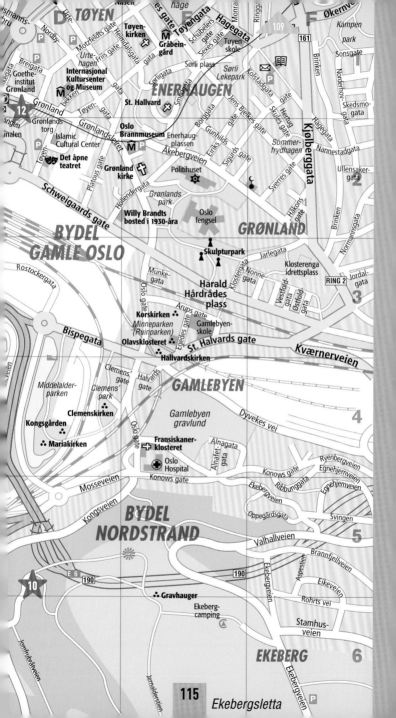

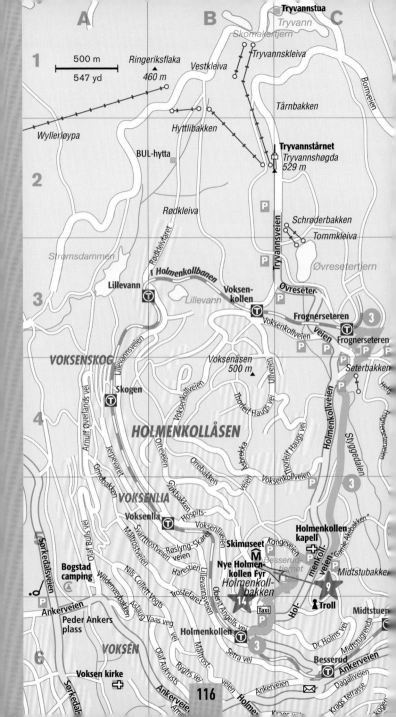

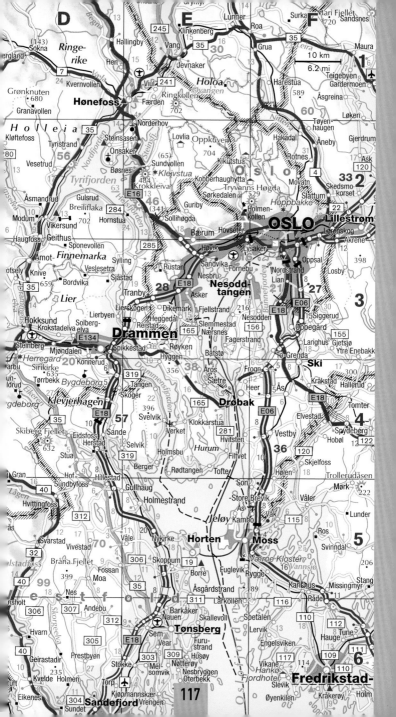

This index lists a selection of the streets and squares shown in the street atlas

KEY TO STREET ATLAS

Ṁ	Museum
🎭	Stage
ⓘ	Information
✝ ⚲ ☦	Church, chapel
✡	Synagogue
☪	Mosque
✚	Hospital
✪	Police
✉	Post
📖	Library
⚊	Monument
∴	Ruin
⚑	Lighthouse
🎾	Tenniscourt
↗	Beach
☀ ☀	Viewpoint
🐘	Zoo
☾	Camping
P P	Parking
⚠	Youth Hostel
⌂ ⌐	Indoor swimming pool, swimming pool
–Ⓣ–	Metro with station
▨	Remarkable building
▨	Public building
▨	Green
▢	Uncovered area
▨▨▨	Pedestrian zone
▬▬▬	Walking tours
⭐1	Marco Polo Highlights

INDEX

This index lists all sights, museums, and destinations, plus the names of important people and key words featured in this guide. Numbers in bold indicate a main entry

SYMBOLS

INSIDER TIP	Insider Tip
★	Highlight
●●●●	Best of ...
☼	Scenic view
☺	Responsible travel: fair trade principles and the environment respected

PRICE CATEGORIES HOTELS

Expensive	over 1100 kroner
Moderate	750–1100 kroner
Budget	under 750 kroner

The prices are for a double room per night including breakfast

PRICE CATEGORIES RESTAURANTS

Expensive	over 220 kroner
Moderate	150–220 kroner
Budget	under 150 kroner

The prices are for a main course without drinks

On the cover: Picnic on the 'iceberg' p. 46 | Trendy Grønland p. 16, 44

MARCO  POLO

Travel with Insider Tips

OSLO

Norwegian Sea

ATLANTIC

OCEAN

NORWAY

SWEDEN

FINLAND

Helsinki

Oslo　Stockholm

GREAT BRITAIN

ESTONIA

LATVIA

DENMARK

LITHUANIA

GERMANY

RUSSIA

NL

POLAND

Hamburg

www.marco-polo.com